The Four Pillars
of Endpoint Security

Dan Griffin

DEDICATION

To my four children: Willow, Branson, Avery, and Molly.

CONTENTS

Overview and Concepts 1

   1   Security Is An Advantage 2

   2   The Four Pillars 5

   3   BYOD Security 10

   4   Keeping Pace With Mobile Computing 14

   5   Security and The Four Pillars 18

Endpoint Hardening 21

   6   Trusted Platform Modules 22

   7   BitLocker Drive Encryption......................................25

   8   Securing Data With BitLocker 29

   9   Securing Your Browsers 31

   10   Hardening Mobile Phones..32

   11   Cloud Security and Mobility 35

   12   Hardening With The Firewall 40

Endpoint Resiliency 57

   13   Reducing Attacks...58

Network Prioritization 61

   14   Trusted Boot 62

   15   More On Measured Boot 67

16   Securing Resources 70

Network Resiliency 74

17   Network Access Protection 75

18   Securing Your Passwords 89

19   One-Time Passwords...90

Conclusion 107

20   Economics and Risk...108

21   From Four Tenets To Four Pillars 116

About The Author 117

ACKNOWLEDGMENTS

Thanks to Tom Jones and Erin Russ for their contributions.

OVERVIEW AND CONCEPTS

1 SECURITY IS AN ADVANTAGE

The Four Pillars of Endpoint Security is a model for making IT security a strategic business asset. Why is this important? Because the most competitive companies want their employees to be productive on their own terms: whenever, wherever, and from whatever device. The best people—the ones you most want to hire and retain—are exactly the ones that are attracted to flexibility, enablement, and rapid decision making.

The most competitive, high-velocity businesses are built on a strong foundation of information technology. IT capabilities, such as providing low-friction access to data and rapid deployment of the latest line-of-business applications, are necessary ingredients, but these capabilities don't develop overnight. Instead, strategic IT capabilities are created through systematic investment, continuous improvement, and recognizing the strong link between IT and business enablement.

Likewise, strategic IT capabilities are built on a foundation of security. If sensitive data can't be protected, one of two things will happen. Either the data won't be made available in the situations where employees are most likely to need it (e.g. on the road, at a customer site, or in a critical meeting), or the data will be made available and it will become compromised or exposed to an unauthorized party. Either way, the business suffers.

The good news is that the tools are available to lay a strong foundation of IT security and to enable the business. The Four Pillars of Endpoint Security provide an easy-to-use context for evaluating and prioritizing the use of those tools.

The Four Tenets of Security

Cloud computing has changed some things like scalability and the cost model for web application hosting. But when it comes to security, the basics still apply. There are four tenets of security: identity, authentication, access control, and authorization.

1. **Identity**—how principals, such as users, are represented.

2. **Authentication**—how identity is established. For example, a user in possession of a smartcard provisioned with a trusted X.509 certificate, plus knowledge of the smartcard PIN, will use the card

to authenticate, thereby establishing his or her identity within the system.

3. **Access control**—the ability of the system to selectively allow or deny principals to perform actions on protected objects. Access control enforces authorization rules.

4. **Authorization**—the process by which access control rules are expressed.

To better understand these four tenets, imagine this: Airbus and Boeing are collaborating on a new Joint Strike Fighter (JSF). Rather than exchange huge engineering design documents between worldwide teams every night, which is what projects of that scale used to entail, the teams collaborate by using a more modern and manageable mix of:

- Centralized document repositories, such as SharePoint.

- Security token server, such as Microsoft Active Directory Federation Services (ADFS) or Shibboleth.

- Password-based and multi-factor authentication technologies, such as smartcard or one-time password (OTP).

In the case of identity, within Airbus' Active Directory (AD) domain, users are represented as security identifiers (SIDs). But those SIDs may have no meaning in Boeing's AD. So identity might be represented by user email address plus other metadata, such as project group membership. And in the case of authorization, it may be necessary to define authorization rules granting auditing staff read-only access to documents on cost expenditures and accounting staff read/write access to those documents.

In order to support complex, collaborative projects such as a design of a JSF, security software has become increasingly complex. For example, the most sensitive data may only be accessible to users with specified project group membership, with certain national citizenship, and from provably secure client hardware. But how do you define an authorization language that allows such rules to be expressed by a typical system administrator? The rules can get even more complex: suppose Airbus trusts identity data regarding JSF weapon system group membership originating from Boeing, since Boeing is contributing to that system. But claims regarding propulsion system group membership from Boeing must be ignored, since that subsystem belongs to Airbus.

Looking at the current state of the art, the capability of expressing such rules exists in the form of standardized technologies such as SAML and XACML. While some ramp-up is required, especially when it comes to complex collaborations, sophisticated line-of-business application integration with those standards is available.

2 THE FOUR PILLARS

The Four Pillars of Endpoint Security complement the four tenets discussed in Chapter 1. The basic premise of the Four Pillars of Endpoint Security is to allow the network to perform even while under attack. But what is an endpoint? In this model, an endpoint is any of the following (where the work is actually done): desktops, servers, and mobile devices.

With these assets in mind, the Four Pillars of Endpoint Security include:

1. **Endpoint hardening**—protect the endpoint from attack.

2. **Endpoint resiliency**—make the endpoint auto-healing.

3. **Network prioritization**—guard network bandwidth.

4. **Network resiliency**—make the network auto-healing.

THE FOUR PILLARS

ENDPOINT
HARDENING

ENDPOINT
RESILIENCY

NETWORK
PRIORITIZATION

NETWORK
RESILIENCY

Protect the endpoint from attack.

Make the endpoint auto-healing.

Guard network bandwidth.

Make the network auto-healing.

Endpoint Hardening

The goal of the first pillar—endpoint hardening—is to ensure that network assets are using the latest technologies to defend against threats. Typical threats include unsafe email attachments, worm-like viruses that propagate over the network, and related threats to your web browsers.

One example of an attack counter-measure is the isolation, or sandboxing, of computer application processes from potential malware by way of mandatory integrity levels enforced by the operating system (OS). This type of protection is applied to Google Chrome and Microsoft Windows. However, manageability can be lacking—namely, the ability to centrally deploy and manage isolation settings for the entire host. In order to be useful, this needs to be done in such a way that third-party applications work seamlessly (and are protected).

How does monitoring apply to this pillar? You should monitor network assets for intrusions in the field in a scalable way. You should also watch for unexpected behavior patterns. The following technologies can aid in endpoint hardening:

- Antivirus and anti-malware software

- Mandatory integrity levels

- Auditing of network resource access

Endpoint Resiliency

The goal of endpoint resiliency is to ensure that health information on devices and applications is continuously gathered and monitored. That way failed devices or applications can be automatically repaired, thus allowing operations to continue. The following technologies can make endpoints more resilient:

- Network access control (NAC), including products such as Cisco NAC and Microsoft Network Access Protection

- Configuration baselining, including the use of government standards such as Security Content Automation Protocol (SCAP)

- Patching

- Antivirus and anti-malware software

- Centralized policy and confirmation management, including products such as Microsoft System Center and VMware vCenter

An open area of development in this space is the need to marry these technologies to produce auto-healing behavior based on standardized, easy-to-extend baselines.

How does monitoring apply to this pillar? Consider trends in any of the following areas:

- Which machines are out of compliance?

- In what way are they non-compliant?

- When is this non-compliant state occurring?

All of these trends can lead to conclusions about potential threats, whether an internal threat, an external threat, a configuration error, user error, and so on. Also, when you identify threats in this manner, you can continuously make endpoints more robust in the face of increasingly sophisticated and distributed attacks.

Network Prioritization

The goal of network prioritization is to ensure that your infrastructure can always meet application bandwidth needs. This consideration applies not only at well-known peak demand times, but also when there are unexpected surges on network loads and distributed external and internal attacks.

Technologies that can manage application bandwidth include DiffServ and Quality of Service (QoS). However, this pillar currently represents the biggest technology gap between what's needed and what's commercially available. In the future, it would help to have solutions to integrate user identity, application identity, and business priorities. Then network routers could automatically partition bandwidth based on that information.

How does monitoring apply to this pillar? Network routers should be doing the flow logging for trend analysis, and effective and comprehensive monitoring can help provide answers to these questions:

- How are today's flows different from yesterday's?

- Is there an increased load?

- What new addresses are involved?

- Is the new traffic originating overseas?

Network Resiliency

The goal of network resiliency is to allow for seamless asset failover. Techniques in this area ideally afford reconfiguring the network in real-time as performance degrades. This pillar is similar to endpoint resiliency in that the goal is to facilitate network self-healing in order to minimize the management burden.

This pillar also draws attention to the fact that failover and redundancy must be considered on a large scale, as well as a small scale. For example, you can use clustering technology to provide failover of a single node within a datacenter, but how do you provide failover for an entire datacenter or region? And the challenge with disaster recovery planning is broader still, because you must also consider office space, basic services and, most importantly, staffing.

In addition to clustering, other relevant technologies under this pillar include replication and virtualization. How does monitoring apply to this pillar? Failover technologies in general rely on monitoring. Plus, you can use load data for resource and acquisition planning as business needs evolve.

Fulfilling the Four Pillars

For each of these Four Pillars of Endpoint Security, there are likely to be commercially available security, network, and business-continuity technologies that are either underutilized or not yet deployed by most organizations. Thus, you as an IT manager have the following opportunities:

- Use the Four Pillars, or some other framework, to identify threats and gaps in your network defenses

- Make additional investments in automation and monitoring

- Engage more closely with business decision makers on the costs and benefits of these efforts

Some enterprises may already find themselves on the cutting edge of what's readily available in one or more of the pillar areas. Thus, there are plenty of opportunities for the entrepreneur as well. What is critical is to restructure your thinking to accommodate each of these Four Pillars, as each is essential.

3 BYOD SECURITY

Bring your own device (BYOD) is the trend in enterprise IT to rely on users to supply their own computing hardware in the form of smartphones, tablets, and, to a lesser extent, laptops. While there is an ostensible cost savings to be had in capital expenditure, and businesses can realize productivity in making it as convenient as possible for employees to always be connected, BYOD is mostly just a response to an external reality: as smartphones become more capable, consumers use them for almost all computing tasks aside from heavy content creation (e.g. programming, video editing). Plus, while checking work email can be a primary task for a consumer smartphone, the latest generation of users communicate via SMS, Facebook, and Twitter. All of those communication needs are met using public, free apps.

In that context, providing knowledge workers with a separate, corporate-managed, mobile computing device is moot. Nobody needs it.

But if your responsibilities include IT security management or compliance, then you should already be squirming. There's a balance to be struck, and it's unlikely to be the same for any two businesses. On one hand, you have to support the latest communication, collaboration, and information exchange modalities if you want to attract and keep the best people and stay ahead of your competitors. On the other hand, there is a fiduciary obligation to deploy security control systems that, at minimum, help keep honest people honest when it comes to data storage and exchange.

Recent competition in the mobile sector has really paid off for consumers: the latest devices from Apple, Google, and Samsung are incredibly cutting-edge and also incredibly usable. That impressive combination is in fact an inspiration for us security folks. Heterogeneity is hard for the IT security manager, since disparate mobile platforms expose different security controls. Yet, the raw power and extensibility present in these devices means that the sky is the limit, both for the IT security manager in terms of developing and applying controls, as well as for the business manager in terms of dreaming up new scenarios for increasing business capability and velocity.

So what steps do you need to take to secure all those mobile devices for corporate data access? You can use the Four Pillars of Endpoint Security as a guide.

1. **Endpoint hardening**—technologies like platform attestation allow server-side resources to extract high-assurance security

claims from mobile devices. This helps to keep sensitive data off of malware and rootkit infested devices and can also be used to enforce client attributes, such as the use of hardware-based disk encryption. The latest generation of mobile devices supports a variety of high-integrity security features, including TPMs, SIMs, and other hardened cryptographic and data protection features.

2. **Endpoint reliability**—the ability to make mobile devices self-healing is still a work-in-progress, but all of the major platforms have recognized the increased support cost, and negative user experience, that comes from supporting a wide-open application ecosystem in which discerning good software from bad is impossible for the layman. Curated app stores help endpoint reliability, although they don't guarantee it. This is moving in the right direction, but enterprises with sophisticated security needs must still necessarily distinguish between managed (for example, an Active Directory domain-joined laptop) and unmanaged (typical smartphone) devices when it comes to granting information access. Enforcing patching and platform updates is key to maintaining endpoint reliability; technologies exist to do this across all platforms.

3. **Network prioritization**—link encryption is a must-have. All web applications should enforce Transport Layer Security (TLS); all clients support it. Don't waste bandwidth on unencrypted or untrusted requests.

4. **Network reliability**—many of the same proven security technologies and practices apply equally across traditional enterprise computing assets: routers, servers, laptops, and desktops. Don't forget that (a) they need to be utilized and (b) they're constantly increasing in sophistication. This applies whether the assets are mobile, private cloud, or public cloud.

In summary: embrace BYOD, enable your business, and allow your employees to be more productive anywhere and from any device. But don't forget to do your risk management homework.

A BYOD Security Cautionary Tale

Never before has the information worker had so much computing power (e.g. smartphone or tablet) always on hand. And never before has it been as easy for IT to support the business with ready access to the data and tools necessary to enable new revenue sources and faster decision making. The decision to embrace BYOD is an easy one: employees, partners, and vendors are likely already using their own computing devices to communicate and collaborate.

But what can be done to establish and enforce practical data security policies for a fast-changing, heterogeneous computing environment? Take a look at this typical BYOD security cautionary tale.

Widget Co. stores its documents on SharePoint and recently migrated to Office 365. The migration has been a boon to the Widgets business teams: they have more control over the look and feel of their team SharePoint pages, they can support a variety of client devices, and allow remote employees, frequent travelers, and vendors to collaborate. Plus, outsourcing is saving time and money for the in-house IT team, allowing them to focus on more strategic efforts, such as enabling new line-of-business scenarios.

Recently, though, a senior executive, distracted after leaving a meeting in a foreign city regarding a potential merger between Widget Co. and Acme, left his tablet in the back of a taxi. Since he's not sure what documents had been downloaded, or when, it's tough to assess the potential impact of the unauthorized data disclosure if the device falls into the wrong hands. Either way, the timing of the loss couldn't be worse: if Acme, its competitors, or even members of the foreign government were to learn details about Widget Co.'s internal discussions about the proposed merger, it could put Widget Co. in a bad place, and likely result in the termination of the executives leading the effort.

Next Steps for the Business Decision Maker

What can the business decision maker (BDM) do to avoid this scenario? The first recommendation may come as a surprise, but this is the real opportunity for the decision maker: don't miss out on the opportunity to enable "anywhere" data access. Wherever your employees happen to be, and whatever device they happen to be using, consider how to let them be most productive. That doesn't mean throw the barn doors wide open to your most sensitive corporate assets. Instead, it means make a reasonable plan for taking advantage of the latest collaborative tools, cloud services, and the security controls they provide. If you don't, your competitors will be moving more quickly than you to enable faster decision making, new lines of business, and even attracting better and brighter employees who thrive in a more dynamic environment. First and foremost, the focus of the BDM must be on enabling the business.

The second recommendation is where risk mitigation comes into play: with the business goals in mind, work with your CIO, CISO, and IT team to establish data security policies to enable them. Make sure the basics are being covered: user authentication, authorization, auditing, and data encryption. In other words, who should have access, and to what? How are those rules being verified? And how can we protect sensitive data—whether in the cloud, on premise, on the move, or in the back of a taxi—and still foster a competitive, collaborative environment that keeps us ahead of the competition?

The most competitive businesses are constantly looking for ways to gain new advantage from their existing IT investments. Look to IT security to be a business enabler. The latest enterprise software tools and cloud services enable more sophisticated security controls than any previous technology generation—use them!

BYOD Security: A Happy Ending

Returning to the example of Widget Co., suppose these data loss prevention policies are established across all IT applications:

- Data is encrypted at rest and in transit

- All mobile devices require password/PIN unlock

With those policies enforced, the lost tablet of the senior executive is a non-issue, the strategic merger between Widget Co. and Acme stays on course, employees stay productive, and the business prospers!

4 KEEPING PACE WITH MOBILE COMPUTING

CNN/Money ran an interesting article entitled "Microsoft is a Dying Consumer Brand" (http://tinyurl.com/239fpc3). Although clearly intended to be provocative, the piece provides a reasonable summary of the challenges faced by several of the relatively older technology companies as they face each other, as well as a long list of newcomers, in the marketplace. While many of these brands have consumer culture in their DNA, several have branched out with enterprise offerings in response to a continuously changing landscape of demand and adoption. In short, diversification is good, but being behind the curve is bad.

Many people believe that mobile computing market-share is critical because the predominant mobile platform influences choice in enterprise computing purchases. While it's difficult to argue against that point, it's also a little slippery. It's something that sounds so obvious when you hear it that you don't bother questioning it.

One thing is clear: the mobile computing market, including handsets and tablets, is going to continue to be one of the primary technology market growth areas for the foreseeable future. Thus, any technology company whose strategy is platform dominance can hardly afford to fail in the mobile space.

There are two important things to keep in mind. First, most of the growth in the mobile computing market is and will be overseas. Microsoft and Apple are good examples of this: both companies have recognized for years that most of the growth in all of their businesses will come from outside the United States.

The second thing to keep in mind is that mobile isn't the only growth area in technology. Services is another. Lotus Notes creator and former Microsoft CTO, Ray Ozzie, made this point very well in his "Dawn of a New Day" blog post (http://tinyurl.com/334esqb). Indeed, smartphones are only as compelling as the connected applications available for them, and those applications can be viewed as services that require a cloud platform to run them. Microsoft has made a significant investment in the Windows Azure cloud platform, as well as in complementary efforts like Office 365. Likewise from Google, with Android on the client and App Engine in the cloud, and from Amazon, with Kindle (running Android) as the client and Amazon Web Services in the cloud.

It's through the lens of this service-connected devices strategy, which Ray Ozzie talks about in his blog post, that you can see that mobile platform dominance is still anyone's game to win. But more importantly, this mobile-plus-cloud strategy is a big signpost guiding IT managers to where they should look for the next wave of innovative tools that can be used for competitive advantage, even if many of the technologies are being marketed first to consumers rather than to enterprise customers. Cloud computing is hardly new news (see *Cloud Security and Control* here: http://tinyurl.com/9zdmqp4). But best practice strategies for enabling a mobile workforce—exposing enterprise data on the Internet to consumer devices, and in a manageable way—remain a fast moving target.

The good news is that, with the service-connected devices strategy in mind, technology providers are making significant investments in the infrastructure and application frameworks that allow valuable data to be exposed without undue risk to downstream revenue opportunities. Even better, because of the advances in the underlying infrastructure that enables cloud computing, these new capabilities are an order of magnitude quicker to deploy, and cheaper to procure and operate, than the previous generation.

Enterprise-facing, service-connected device solutions are still in their infancy, however. This partly relates to the aforementioned risk that the big technology vendors see in losing the initial battle for consumer mindshare with mobile devices: the predominant strategy for hardware vendors, at least, is to focus on consumers first. That service-connected device technologies are evolving so quickly is also due to the relatively sudden and rapid mainstream adoption of smartphones and tablets.

For the enterprise IT manager, the service-connected device strategy is a double-edged sword. On one hand, investment in specific mobile and cloud technologies and tools may rapidly become obsolete. On the other hand, improving the capability of quickly absorbing and combining new technologies, integrating them into an organization's existing methodology and processes, is a safe, long-term investment. The biggest risk from an endpoint security standpoint is likely to be underinvestment in capabilities that allow employees to be productive anywhere, from any device.

The following technologies enable and embody the service-connected device strategy:

- Laptop LoJack (http://tinyurl.com/8du8vk7)

- SecurEntity (http://tinyurl.com/8xs869r)

- StrongNet (http://tinyurl.com/9z8ky6n)

The first tenet of the JW Secure StrongNet initiative is Endpoint Hardening, which consists of defensive technologies that protect servers and workstations from malware and network-based attacks.

Microsoft's Scott Charney talked about endpoint health in his RSA 2011 keynote speech (http://tinyurl.com/dxxqwf9). Specifically, he showed a demo in which a user is blocked from signing in to a sensitive website, such as online banking, if the client PC is missing up-to-date anti-malware defense.

Additionally, NSA announced its High Assurance Platform (HAP) program (http://tinyurl.com/8zqg4a3). HAP consists of a multi-level security system based on attestation and secure domain separation. In summary, attestation is provided by a Trusted Platform Module (TPM) based trusted boot. Secure domain separation is provided by a hypervisor (specifically, VMware's) and virtualization.

Other good references for building systems using these technologies include:

- "Advanced Persistent Threats Mitigation Best Practices" whitepaper from TSCP (http://tinyurl.com/98h6pe6)

- BIOS Protection Guidelines from NIST (http://tinyurl.com/3ekvoaw)

Endpoint Security and the Consumerization of IT

The proliferation of smartphones and tablets has created a population of users that have come to expect that they can have immediate access to any data anywhere that they might be. The popularity of smartphones led to their sales exceeding all PCs in 2011, and that was before the impact of tablet computing had really taken off. Every public location that encourages users to linger provides Wi-Fi access, otherwise customers look elsewhere for a coffee and a connection.

In the enterprise, the pressure to enable fully mobile access to corporate resources is significant. Enterprise IT needs to get out in front of this trend in order to support mobile access in an orderly and secure manner, since users are inevitably pushing for quicker adoption than can be safely deployed for certain key applications. And this encompasses support across the full spectrum of applications: today's pressure to enable email and sharing will morph into tomorrow's demand for mobile access to systems used for SCADA and national defense.

What kind of mobile devices will IT support?

The U.S. Department of Defense found that the mobile communications of their warfighters in the Middle East was badly outclassed by the insurgents using cellular phones for both intelligence and triggering bombs. Enterprise IT departments are facing a similar gap between their services and public experience with consumer online service. While the consumer driven approach championed by Apple and Android is dominant today, look for enterprise-class security features to become increasingly important in the coming device generations.

5 SECURITY AND THE FOUR PILLARS

The basic premise of the Four Pillars of Endpoint Security is to enable the business: when data security assurance can be made, then the data can be made available; and when the data is available, it can best serve your decision makers.

For each pillar, there are several additional goals to consider:

- It's advisable to automate the process as much as possible. After all, there are only so many hours in the day, and IT managers already have full schedules.

- You should centrally monitor your network so you know what's happening in real-time. While one purpose of the two resiliency pillars is to reduce this monitoring burden as much as possible, sometimes you have to implement manual defenses and counter-measures. Also, equipment sometimes fails even under normal conditions.

- Establish a feedback loop. As attacks become increasingly sophisticated, you must acknowledge that your defenses won't keep up unless you continuously make the right investments to shore them up. At the same time, you must recognize that investments in network security have historically proven to be tough to justify as critical business expenses.

This is why constant monitoring and feedback is essential. The better you understand—and can demonstrate—the actual threats and attacks occurring at your perimeter and within the network, the better you can justify the attention and expense paid to protecting those business assets.

The Four Pillars Mean Compliance

Every enterprise has compliance criteria that have been imposed by internal or external regulations. The deployment of a new device technology does not free IT from compliance requirements. New devices must be adapted to the existing requirements. The Four Pillars of Endpoint Security were developed to focus on the best practices for applying controls and achieving compliance.

To put this into context, let's look at the recent distributed denial of service attacks by Iran on several U.S. banks. The attacks made use of large botnets, or compromised Internet-connected computers, from all over the globe. By applying The Four Pillars of Endpoint Security to this scenario, it looks like this:

1. **Endpoint hardening**—make client operating systems harder to compromise and incorporate into botnets. Secondarily, one hopes that server operating systems can be made more capable to resist DDoS attacks.

2. **Endpoint reliability**—ensure that compromised botnet hosts should self-heal. Why not? The bot behavior is anomalous, and hardware enforcement of known-good system software is available.

3. **Network prioritization**—throttle hosts that don't have authorization to send certain traffic to certain servers. For example, there are countries from which network traffic destined for U.S. banks should be completely and permanently blocked as a matter of national security. That doesn't mitigate the risk from compromised U.S.-based hosts, but it reduces the effective size of the botnet.

4. **Network reliability**—ensure that networks themselves, including dedicated firewall equipment, continue to perform in the face of brutal traffic spikes. In addition, network reliability is an important consideration for user-friendly mobile and web application design. Good mobile-app design, using techniques such as data caching and tiered access, can make outages feel more seamless.

The Four Pillars of Endpoint Security complement other IT process management methodologies well. For more, see the lifecycle management and continuous improvement tactics employed by the following:

- Capability Maturity Model Integration (CMMI) (http://tinyurl.com/yrrfn)

- Control Objectives for Information and Related Technologies (CoBIT) (http://tinyurl.com/ccgdu7g)

- Microsoft Operations Framework (MOF) (http://tinyurl.com/8crjqeb)

- Information Technology – Information Security – Information Assurance (ISACA) (http://tinyurl.com/33xmyse)

ENDPOINT HARDENING

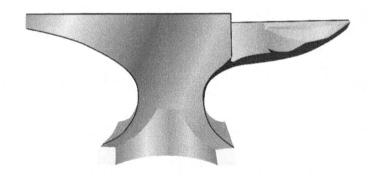

6 TRUSTED PLATFORM MODULES

What is it about networked computers that allow them to be so easily hacked? A weakness that is frequently exploited by malware writers involves the conversion of web content, attractively displayed for the casual user, into a set of instructions that undermines the browser.

John von Neumann invented general purpose computers by putting both data and code on the same memory bus. This was an advance over earlier designs but it opened the door for malware: malicious code can be inserted into an area of the computer memory used for data storage and the computer can then be fooled into running that malware. From the moment that a document becomes an unwanted source of computer instructions, all data that is accessible by the computer is also accessible by the malware.

Generally, blocking malware from execution has proven to be difficult to achieve. However, there is one method that uses a hardware-protected part of the computer to hold secret cryptographic material that can tell us when the computer has been successfully contaminated by malware.

Many PCs are fitted with a Trusted Platform Module (TPM) that enables a cryptographic statement to be made about the security disposition of the computer. That statement can be transmitted to a remote server (or, remote attestation) in order to assure that the computer can be relied on to faithfully keep secrets such as your identity or credit card numbers. The value of remote attestation is hard to overstate since it blocks much of the value that malware writers earn for their efforts. If users quickly learn that their computers have been compromised, and they are blocked from performing valuable transactions until the computer is fixed, the window of opportunity for the malware writer to take advantage of the compromised computer narrows.

TRUSTED PLATFORM MODULE

PCRs

Crypto Engine

Key Storage

So how can security be made usable enough that users will consider it to be an ally rather than an annoying obstacle? In the case of the TPM, two new developments are converging. In most cases the owners of those computers neither have the time, expertise, nor desire to get the same security level that is enjoyed by employees in large, security-minded enterprises. But soon the Trusted Computer Group will be publishing a new standard implementation of a TPM on a thin hardware layer like the ARM Trust Zone, which has been shipping in smartphones for several years. At the same time, it's expected that the release of Windows 8 on ARM and x86 architectures will have a requirement for TPM support. These two coming events will bring the possibility of simplified provisioning of the TPM even for consumer services.

JW Secure has been building support systems for TPM-use with data protection for several years, and now is working on a simplified method that allows users to pick up a computer at their local superstore and securely provision it anywhere.

The following websites describe more about the capabilities of the TPM, its use, and the increasing number of devices supporting it:

- NSA High Assurance Platform (http://tinyurl.com/d7uyr98)

- Trusted Platform Group (TCG) focus on real-world data protection (http://tinyurl.com/cb8ufjw)

- Windows 8 Logo Program to Require TPM 2.0 solution on computers (http://tinyurl.com/8yobshf)

7 BITLOCKER DRIVE ENCRYPTION

If you search the Internet for "stolen hard drive," you'll get a reminder of how at-risk your data is, and how visible and embarrassing the loss or theft of sensitive data can be, especially if the event is covered by the press. The loss of corporate data can also cause damage to your brand and confer an advantage to your competitors if trade secrets are revealed.

In many cases, encryption of customer data is required by law. For example, the PCI Data Security Standard for the credit card industry, and the Health Insurance Portability and Accountability Act (HIPAA) for the healthcare industry both require encryption of certain end-user data (e.g. personally identifiable information [PII], credit card numbers, and patient records). Corporate risk officers should also be aware that regulations, such as the California data breach notification law, require disclosure only if the lost data is not encrypted.

With BitLocker Drive Encryption, you can help protect your company from these threats. BitLocker encrypts an entire disk volume. Under the hood, the encrypted volume is protected by the volume master key, which in turn is encrypted by an administrator selected key protector. For more information about the keys and how encryption works, see the BitLocker technical overview (http://tinyurl.com/ceot2zu).

Note that while the volume master key must be available in order for the encrypted drive to be used, the security of the encryption is only as strong as the protection that you apply to the volume master key. To put it another way, the volume master key must be encrypted in such a way that good guys can decrypt it but bad guys can't. Meeting this interesting challenge is the purpose of key protectors.

How BitLocker Works with Windows

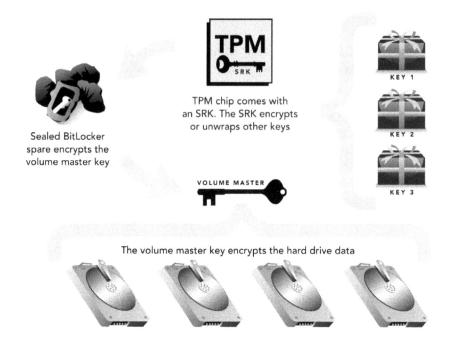

TPM chip comes with an SRK. The SRK encrypts or unwraps other keys

KEY 1

KEY 2

KEY 3

Sealed BitLocker spare encrypts the volume master key

VOLUME MASTER

The volume master key encrypts the hard drive data

Key Protectors

There are several key protectors that an administrator can select, and a well-planned deployment will use specific combinations of key protectors depending on whether the host is mobile (a laptop) or stationary (a server).

Security

From a security perspective, the most important key protectors are the ones that make use of the Trusted Platform Module (TPM). As discussed in Chapter 6, Trusted Platform Modules, the TPM is a tamper-resistant chip embedded in the motherboard of most modern enterprise-class PCs. The qualifiers in the previous sentence are inevitably a source of complexity for a BitLocker deployment. For example, what policies should you set for older PCs that don't have a TPM? This is still a hard problem to solve, and requires custom scripting.

The TPM is critical for BitLocker since it allows the volume master key to be bound to a specific PC. If data theft is the goal, removal of a hard drive (e.g. from a server room) is the most common way to accomplish it; the attacker can then attach the drive to another PC and copy the data. However, if the encrypted volumes on the drive are using a TPM as the key protector, the attacker can't decrypt the volumes without having physical access to the original PC. If the original PC is still in the server room, the good guys win: there's no way for the attacker to compromise the data without a brute-force attack.

Not all machines are difficult to steal, though. Laptops are increasingly popular in the workplace, and sensitive data is often stored on them. To ensure that the bad guys don't get that data on the encrypted drive, it's important to use the TPM plus a boot PIN. The boot PIN must be entered each time the system boots. (Yes, your users will complain, but the extra security is worth it.) This key protector combination reduces the threat of Direct Memory Access (DMA) attacks. The Microsoft BitLocker team wrote a good blog post on DMA and other related attacks, which sums up the threat very well (http://tinyurl.com/28chtsl).

To summarize the attack, some PC peripherals allow DMA for performance reasons, but this configuration could allow an attacker to use a DMA device to read the contents of the PC memory without having to log on. If those memory contents happen to include sensitive information, then BitLocker has effectively been bypassed. However, with a boot PIN, the attacker cannot even boot the machine in the first place (without knowing the PIN). Still, it's important to recognize that if a laptop is already booted when it's stolen, or if the target is a running server, DMA attacks are still a threat. To mitigate this threat, as described in the blog post mentioned above, DMA-capable devices, including 1394 and PCI bus-attached, can be disabled.

Data Recovery

The Numeric Password allows the volume master key to be archived in Active Directory, which makes it the most important key protector for ensuring that you can reliably recover your users' data. There are two situations that can necessitate key recovery: a forgotten boot PIN and a change in hardware.

First, as any system administrator knows, it is inevitable that a user will forget the boot PIN. And while BitLocker allows a recovery key to be saved to a USB token, it can certainly be lost as well. Therefore, since the data doesn't do you much good if you can't decrypt it, centrally managed archival of recovery keys is important for preventing data loss.

Second, using the strong protection afforded by the TPM is a tradeoff. While the TPM does a great job of detecting the types of hardware changes that might indicate that it was removed or is under attack, those same features make it sensitive to some hardware changes that are otherwise benign. A change to the boot device on the host PC is an example. This is another scenario in which Active Directory-based recovery key storage can save you.

8 SECURING DATA WITH BITLOCKER

Configuring Mobile Assets for BitLocker

There are two classes of mobile assets that you should consider when planning your data protection scheme. The first class is portable USB keys and drives. It is recommended that you protect those using BitLocker To Go, which is available in the Enterprise and Ultimate editions of Windows 7, in Windows 8 Pro, Windows Server 2008 R2, and Windows Server 2012.

The second class of mobile assets is laptops. Use the following BitLocker configuration on your organization's laptops:

- Numeric Password key protector, along with Active Directory archival

- TPM + PIN key protector

Configuring Non-Mobile Assets for BitLocker

The recommended BitLocker configuration for servers and workstations is similar to that of laptops. The difference is that you generally don't want to require a boot PIN for these non-mobile assets. A boot PIN can still be used if you desire, but the tradeoff is that every time the machine reboots, someone must be present at the console to type in the PIN. For servers, that's generally an unacceptable tradeoff. Therefore the following BitLocker configuration for servers and workstations is more secure:

- Numeric Password key protector, along with Active Directory archival

- TPM key protector

Policy Enforcement

The primary shortcoming to be aware of when rolling out BitLocker is that there's currently no way to enforce the drive encryption process, which means that you'll need to write a script for encrypting the drive. When writing a script, you can use either the BitLocker WMI provider or the manage-bde command-line tool.

The following references on TechNet provide more information:

- Advanced configuration options for BitLocker
  (http://tinyurl.com/8bgdnnn)

- BitLocker WMI provider (http://tinyurl.com/8k2rmqc)

- Manage-bde command-line tool (http://tinyurl.com/8hm5x8p)

Compliance Reporting

Similar to policy enforcement, compliance reporting is an important aspect of a BitLocker deployment, but is unfortunately not directly supported out-of-the-box, which means that you'll have to write scripts to get compliance reporting working properly. When writing your script, consider using a logon script to check the BitLocker status, and then write the results to a file share or web service.

Microsoft's software-based disk encryption technology, BitLocker, has a new competitor in the form of self-encrypting drives. Notably, those drives don't require a TPM security chip on the motherboard or the premium Windows SKU that Microsoft requires for BitLocker, both of which increase the cost of deployment. There are some important tradeoffs, though, which impact both security and the total cost of ownership.

9 SECURING YOUR BROWSERS

Internet browsers have had it tough lately. A few years ago, the German government warned against using Internet Explorer, and then they warned against using Firefox. Shortly thereafter, another zero-day security flaw in Internet Explorer was announced on March 20, 2010 (http://tinyurl.com/cyypxg8). Similar vulnerabilities are found each year in most browsers.

The bottom line: there's no way to browse with 100% safety. But don't give up. Follow these guidelines and you'll be more secure:

- Always use the latest browser version and operating system platform, whether it's Internet Explorer, Firefox or Chrome

- Always keep your patches up-to-date

- Browse as a standard/regular user—that is, not as a member of the local Administrators group

- Don't browse to sites you don't know

- Don't click on ads

- Don't install software off the web

- Use a different password for each site

Of all of those, the last one is usually the most difficult to achieve. The best solution for remembering so many different passwords: don't try. Instead, write them all down on a piece of paper and keep it in your purse or wallet. Chapter 18, Securing Your Passwords, goes into more detail about this.

10 HARDENING MOBILE PHONES

In September 2011, AVG released the first antivirus application for Windows Phone 7 (http://tinyurl.com/8v7a7wm). However, the public programming model for Windows Phone 7 is relatively restrictive when compared to Android, for example. Therefore, there's little AVG can do in terms of real security checks (http://tinyurl.com/3vev7h4). Microsoft allows only the mobile carriers (i.e. companies that sign big expensive licensing deals) to have access to the full capabilities of the phone operating system. The rest of the world, including companies like AVG, can only produce simple app-store applications, such as web-based games.

This arrangement is limiting, particularly if you're a software company trying to do something other than gaming. Antivirus is a great example of that. Plus, even though Windows Phone 7 is a consumer play, employers these days have little choice but to support employee-supplied devices, and hence there's a gap in enterprise capability. That is, many business-related connectivity and productivity scenarios require features above and beyond those currently available in Windows Phone 7 in order to meet a typical bar for IT security, compliance, and manageability.

There's a flipside to Microsoft's strategy there, though. For one thing, simple web-based games, and other utility applications with similar capabilities are what nearly all consumers are expecting to find in an app store. And there's no debating that it's consumers who are making the purchasing decisions here, not employers. In theory, by focusing on the majority case, Microsoft can better compete. Marketplace diversity is good.

It has also been argued that this reduced programmability is actually good for consumer security, since it means that app-store apps are less likely to be able to damage the phone, steal data from other apps, and so on. However, that argument is misleading, since an app-store app can just as easily use social engineering to prompt the user for a password, credit card number, SSN, or other private data, and then do anything with it. Phone apps can also load any website, so all of the usual web-based attacks are possible.

A rich and well supported extensibility model has historically been the competitive strong suit of Microsoft's platforms. The current Windows Phone 7 strategy notwithstanding, that aspect of the market does not seem to have changed. Android itself is proof of that.

Mobile Device Best Practices

By applying the Four Pillars of Endpoint Security strategy, you can focus on key areas of investment to enable the business to operate without interruption.

Endpoint hardening options for mobile devices shipping today are limited but are improving. Exchange ActiveSync is one example of a set of security policies with good cross-platform support. Platform-specific options are also being developed. Several vendors are working on hardened Android solution for use in national defense roles. In addition, both Windows Phone 8 and Windows RT will also include enhanced security features, such as the Trusted Platform Module (TPM), giving devices running those operating systems a strong data security story.

Endpoint reliability for mobile devices is all about detecting the health of the device and initiating remediation when it is out of compliance with the corporate security policy. An important class of products for enabling endpoint reliability is antivirus and anti-malware software. As above, enterprise-class solutions are still playing catch-up, even on the dominant mobile platforms. But antivirus mobile apps are available from reputable vendors, and it's recommended that you use them.

Network prioritization is best captured by this goal: optimize the user experience. An example is the use of flow-control to enable real-time delivery of audio and visual content and to enable high bandwidth utilization. The proliferation of a wide variety of screen resolutions, and a diverse set of client operating systems running on highly capable hardware, introduces a new wrinkle here since part of enabling efficient network utilization is to ensure that content delivery matches the device capabilities. In order to achieve this, both websites and apps must be designed to be responsive.

Network reliability for mobile devices is often touted as high, but anyone who uses a smartphone and data connection has no doubt experienced the inconvenience of spotty coverage. The best apps are those that can provide value offline in these conditions and then seamlessly return to connectivity once the network is again available.

You can embrace mobile computing in the enterprise, but don't forget to follow these security best practices:

- Catalog and review compliance criteria to see if they are jeopardized by mobile devices or network access

- Determine and document the policy for each type of mobile device and app that you will support

- Create a plan to enable and enforce hardware protection of data on mobile devices

- Ensure that data on remote devices will be made inaccessible when a device is reported lost or when an employee leaves the enterprise

- Create a plan for websites to use a single data model with views that are responsive to each device type

11 CLOUD SECURITY AND MOBILITY

Imagine that you need to develop a mobile dashboard for patient healthcare data. The dashboard must address the following requirements:

1. Allow in-house healthcare providers to access an up-to-date summary of the patient history. Healthcare providers must be able to view this summary using a standard smartphone.

2. Allow external healthcare providers, such as a team of radiologists in India, to access patient data when they are interpreting imagery data in support of a 24-hour productivity cycle.

3. Be as close as possible to Health Insurance Portability and Accountability Act (HIPAA) compliance, including meeting requirements for auditing and data encryption.

These requirements present plenty of challenges. While sharing the data externally necessitates federation and a cloud-based solution, compliance and cloud computing don't necessarily happily coexist. In addition, medical imagery files are large. Finally, healthcare providers are often wary of adopting new technologies in the workplace since some past implementations might have slowed them down.

However, for rapid development and deployment of a mobile application using federated authentication, the cloud is often still the fastest and most cost-effective option available. For an independent software vendor (ISV), being the first-to-market may be crucial for the success of the solution. For an internal IT team, there is inexorable pressure to cut costs. However, the flexibility of the cloud makes it easier to deliver a new and compelling application online, on schedule, and cost-effectively.

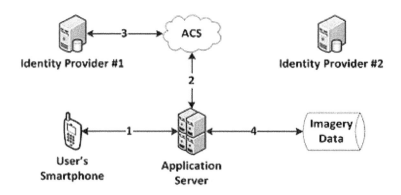

Figure 1 Application components

For reference, Figure 1 identifies the major data flows.

1. The user launches the application.

2. In order to perform authentication, the application server redirects the client to a Security Token Service (STS), such as Windows Azure AppFabric Access Control Service (ACS).

3. ACS redirects the user to the appropriate identity provider. In this case, that is the Active Directory Federation Services (ADFS) server operated by the user's employer.

4. Once authentication and authorization are successfully completed, the user may access the requested application data. The data access is audited by the application server.

Note that the Identity Provider #2 server in the diagram is included to illustrate how an external team (e.g. the off-site radiology team in India) could securely access the imagery data, as well. In this instance, the accounts for the off-site team are stored in Active Directory. See the Authentication section below for more details about this scenario.

Compliance

In regard to technical security requirements, the main issue to consider is compliance. For example, we know that patient data has to be encrypted, that we must put controls in place to prevent accidental disclosure, and that we need to audit access.

Authentication

Users will sign into the mobile application with a username and password. To mitigate the risk of stolen or shared passwords, it is recommended that you use a multifactor authentication method, such as username/password and radio frequency identification (RFID) card combination. However, while the medical field has begun to adopt RFID cards, smartphones generally do not include RFID readers.

One-time Passwords (OTPs) are another multifactor authentication option. Some organizations have become concerned about the security of OTPs after the high-profile attacks against RSA Data Security and some of its customers. However, an OTP solution is still an excellent choice for multifactor authentication, and it is vastly preferable to static passwords. Chapter 19, One-Time Passwords, goes into more detail about this.

Because this scenario involves both on- and off-premises users (e.g. the off-site radiology team in India), you must also support federation of the user accounts. Assume that the on-premises personnel have accounts in Active Directory. The outsourced radiology team will have its own account store, and that store might not be Active Directory–based. Some organizations will choose to create accounts in Active Directory for the outsourced team, while others will choose to trust the outsourced team to be authenticated using its own systems. Either way, in order to expose the on-premises Active Directory accounts to the cloud, you should use ADFS. There might be one or two ADFS servers involved in the scenario—one if the outsourced team is not using Active Directory and two if it is. Identity claims issued by ADFS can be processed either directly by the application service or by a claims mapping service, such as Windows Azure AppFabric ACS.

Authorization and Auditing

The biggest complaint of IT organizations as they transition services to the cloud is loss of control. Claims-based authorization is an under-utilized technique that is relevant in this context because fine-grained control is its primary benefit. One example of claims-based authorization is apparent in the context of the mobile imagery application: if the user is the patient's recorded doctor, he or she can view that patient's imagery data.

Designing the authorization scheme to be used by the mobile imagery application first entails determining which account stores will be trusted to authenticate users. Secondly, it involves establishing requirements about the claims that must be issued by those identity providers in order for authorization decisions to be made. For example, the application may be dependent on a Title claim, with possible values including Doctor and Nurse. It is recommended that you use claims mapping for simplifying this task (http://tinyurl.com/9vlgvsb).

Compliance auditing requirements are another great example of how claims-based authorization can be used to improve control. You can configure the medical imaging application to require the user to present trusted claims not only about the user's account name and title, as described above, but also about the client device. In the case of the mobile device, you will gather information about the device type, unique device ID, firmware version, and even what other user applications are installed. If the user has installed a mobile application determined to be malware, policy can be set in the medical application to strictly audit access or even deny access in order to help ensure that sensitive patient data cannot be compromised by the suspected or known malware.

In fact, more and more information about the health of the client device (in this case, a smartphone) is becoming available. This important and positive trend allows the IT department to effectively offer wider access to data with lower risk. If the server can trust the client to accurately report on its system state, the server can also decide whether the client is sufficiently secure to receive sensitive data. This capability, combined with strong user authentication, allows the IT manager to help ensure that only the right people have access to the right data from the right devices, and still provide access to the users from anywhere in the world. For more information about tracking client health claims, you can read about secure boot and remote attestation on the JW Secure website (http://tinyurl.com/8nypv3q).

For each call into the application server, a range of information about the user and device is available for auditing, as well as for making granular authorization decisions.

Encryption

Several options are available for encrypted data stored in the cloud. The main determining factor in evaluating those options is to decide whether plaintext (unencrypted) data may ever reside in the cloud, even if only briefly. Suppose, for example, that a typical three-tier application architecture is used for the mobile imagery example. The first tier is the mobile device, the second tier is an application server where business logic is implemented, and the third tier is where the data is stored. If the application server resides in the cloud, then there will inevitably be unencrypted data exposed to the cloud since the data must be in plaintext form in order for the application to display it. That's true even if the third tier uses encryption or is stored on-premises. That question—where to host the application tier if sensitive data is in play—is one of the single toughest architectural issues that the IT manager faces when it comes to realizing the cost savings and nimbleness offered by cloud computing.

On the one hand, exceeding the requirements of compliance rarely makes good business sense, and in many situations, the industry standard appears to be to overlook this issue: as long as the data isn't persisted or transmitted in unencrypted form, it's okay for it to exist temporarily in plaintext on the application tier (even though temporary can be tough to define, due to data caching, swap files, and so on).

On the other hand, there are plenty of examples of data that should never touch the cloud in plaintext form, such as highly sensitive or strategic business information, and classified government documents. Therefore, it is important to note that cloud computing benefits can still be realized in those situations. Using an on-premises data encryption proxy, the organization can take advantage of cloud storage while still ensuring that plaintext data never touches the cloud.

For more information about encrypting data on-premises, you can read about cloud data encryption on the JW Secure website (http://tinyurl.com/8z4pydg). And additional information about designing cloud-based healthcare solutions is available in Transforming Care Delivery with Windows Azure (http://tinyurl.com/8ns2wpv).

12 HARDENING WITH THE FIREWALL

Below are pointers to existing documentation and background information that every programmer should peruse, prior to using the Windows Firewall API:

- About the Windows Firewall API (http://tinyurl.com/9jg5qrf)

- Existing Windows Firewall sample code (http://tinyurl.com/8suw6zr)

- Introduction to the Windows Filtering Platform on which the Windows Firewall is based (http://tinyurl.com/8ubdyou)

- The five or so (short) introductory web pages that follow the article in the MSDN table of contents, including the architectural diagram that shows how the Windows Firewall (and a typical socket application) interacts with the filtering platform

This solution demonstrates the use of two closely related Windows APIs: those for the Windows Filtering Platform and those for the Windows Firewall. The Windows Filtering Platform API was originally added to Windows in Windows Vista. While some of the capabilities of the Windows Filtering Platform and Windows Firewall APIs overlap in Windows, it's important to understand the scenarios to which each applies.

But first, an anecdote. My first attempt to add firewall rules programmatically for my sample TCP server was based on the Windows Filtering Platform API. This was partly because I first found a sample in the latest SDK that demonstrates adding Windows Filtering Platform–based rules for MSN Messenger. Because I had no reason to suspect that this wouldn't be a good starting point for my own work, I used it as a baseline. Using the Windows Filtering Platform API instead of the Windows Firewall API was also initially attractive, because I found the Windows Filtering Platform API to be more intuitive.

However, while testing my first Windows Filtering Platform–based solution, I found that, even after adding my filters, I was still getting prompted by the Windows Firewall when the TCP socket-based test-server program started listening on its port. Windows Vista displayed the following dialog box when I was testing my first Windows Filtering Platform-based solution:

Figure 2 Windows Security Alert dialog box in Windows Vista

Furthermore, my Windows Filtering Platform rules seemed to be ignored. If I clicked the Keep blocking button, the client could never connect, regardless of my own filter. If I clicked the Unblock button, the server was able to receive all traffic, regardless of the client address—even though my filter was more restrictive. In other words, despite the presence of my filter, I was still observing the default per-application behavior of the Windows Firewall.

This was contrary to my goals, as I wanted to demonstrate the proper way to install very specific firewall rules and avoid the preceding potentially confusing dialog box.

Subsequent conversation with the engineering team at Microsoft clarified that the Windows Filtering Platform API is not intended to be used in the way in which I was using it. In scenarios in which the Windows Firewall is enabled, and a standard network-based application needs to open one or more ports, the Windows Firewall API should be used. In contrast, the primary purpose of the Windows Filtering Platform API is to facilitate development of rule-based network-infrastructure technologies, such as third-party firewalls. Indeed, the Windows Firewall is based on the Windows Filtering Platform API, as will be demonstrated later in this chapter, and non-Microsoft firewalls also are intended to be so.

You can infer from this situation that it's Microsoft's intent that the average network application should not interact with the Windows Filtering Platform API in any way. Instead, such applications should call into the higher-level Windows Firewall APIs during installation and un-installation. This is best practice, as the Windows Firewall is enabled by default. However, application developers should also provide documentation that details the expected firewall-rules configuration for proper and secure operation. This is important, as the Windows Firewall may have been replaced by a non-Microsoft solution (and, therefore, a different programmatic interface). Finally, this should serve as a gentle reminder that Windows should always have a software firewall enabled and correctly configured.

Sample Business Problem

As in the previous chapters, suppose you work at a large manufacturing enterprise, and that one business group maintains an internal software application that stores customer information, including some sensitive data like credit card and social security numbers. Suppose, further, that to create synergy across the organization, another business group must now have access to the same data.

As the in-house developer in charge of this line-of-business application, suppose that you've been asked to confirm that it's sufficiently robust for the new demands that will be placed on it, including the need for additional users and increased exposure of the sensitive data to the corporate network.

Considering the problem in a somewhat broader sense, depending on the internal network-security policies of the organization, such an application may be hosted on a server that itself is protected by a third-party firewall solution.

The following items may compound the problem:

- Administrative access to the server may be tightly controlled and audited

- The application architecture may be three-tier, with the data hosted off-box

- IPsec policies may be in place to protect network traffic, at least between the application and database servers

These are all good things. However, additional defense-in-depth measures are recommended. To put it another way, as a software developer, you shouldn't assume that security mechanisms beyond your direct control, such as a hardware-based firewall, are present or configured correctly. This is where a discussion of the Windows Firewall becomes interesting. In the context of this example, the objective is to configure the software firewall under the assumption that it's the last defense standing between an army of bad guys and the sensitive customer data. Realistically, leveraging the security mechanisms that are offered by the underlying platform is especially important in light of the fact that many organizations lack the resources to deploy the additional security mechanisms mentioned earlier.

Although the following discussion focuses only on configuring the software firewall, in reality, other aspects of the security design of the application need to be considered. For example, has the code recently undergone a thorough security review?

Sample Solution

It's implied that the application is hosted on Windows Vista or a later version of Windows. A portion of the sample code is based on a pre-existing sample from the Windows Vista version of the Windows SDK (formerly known as the Platform SDK). The original sample code for the TCP server application can be found in the Samples\NetDs\winsock\securesocket subdirectory of the SDK installation. The original code included some logic that pertained to IPsec and IPv6, which has been intentionally disabled or removed in order to limit the scope of this particular discussion. More Windows Firewall–related sample code also accompanies the latest Windows SDK. See the Samples\Security\WindowsFirewall subdirectory.

Firewall Rules

A firewall rule includes configurable conditions for a variety of network-traffic characteristics (ports, addresses, and so on). A rule must specify an action: Allow or Block. Therefore, in order for an Allow rule to apply, each of its conditions must be met.

This is exactly the behavior that is applied in the sample code. Namely, the application is opening a socket on the server and waiting for clients to make requests. By default, the application is listening on a port that is expected to be blocked by the Windows Firewall. The sample code causes the firewall to open that port, but to allow through only network traffic that meets certain conditions. It also makes those conditions as restrictive as possible. Any traffic that doesn't meet every filter condition should never be able to access the application. This is an important security concept; the default answer for inbound packets that want to traverse the firewall, even when your application is listening on its port, is still, "No!"

Ultimately, the appropriate set of filter conditions will vary for each application and deployment. Bearing in mind, again, that the rule or rules should be as restrictive as possible, a representative set of conditions has been created in this example. In this case, it won't accept any traffic, unless it meets all of the following conditions.

1. The protocol in use is TCP/IP. For example, it won't accept UDP traffic.

2. The destination port is the specific one upon which the application is listening.

3. The client address is of an expected range. Given that this example is tested only with IPv4 addresses, this condition is easy to implement for small organizations, especially those that use NAT. In those cases, the client-address condition might stipulate 192.168.1.0 with the corresponding mask of 255.255.255.0. For organizations with multiple noncontiguous address ranges, managing the configuration of this rule is a little tougher, but certainly not impossible.

4. Finally, as an added bonus, ensure that the preceding rule applies only to your specific application, and only when it's running. That is, you don't want another process on the host server to be able to receive your traffic, intentionally or otherwise.

Implementation of the Sample Firewall Rule

As mentioned previously, a Windows Firewall API rule exposes a variety of optional conditions. Programmatically, the conditions are exposed as properties of the INetFwRule interface. In fact, the available set of properties is sufficiently expressive that the desired behavior of the sample socket application can be achieved with a single rule. That's exactly what is hoped for: conceptually, you want to open a port, as well as enable a specific application to listen on it, but only to certain types of traffic. It's easy to imagine how a rules engine that requires two separate rules to implement that behavior might, in fact, not be able to achieve it. For example, the resulting filters could be overly permissive due to a port being open but not bound to a specific application. The next section shows you how to test for such situations.

Here's the code that creates the rule and enables it on the host. The function is WFAddRule, and it is part of the FwTool.exe utility. This utility is discussed in more detail in the Testing section.#import "netfw.tlb"

```
// Add settings for the demo server application to the
Windows Firewall

DWORD
WINAPI
WFAddRule(
    __in        LPWSTR wszServerAppName,
    __in        LPWSTR wszServerAppFullPath,
    __in        LPWSTR wszFirewallGrouping,
    __in        NET_FW_IP_PROTOCOL fwIpProtocol,
    __in        LPWSTR wszRemoteAddresses,
    __in        LPWSTR wszLocalPort)
{
  HRESULT hr = S_OK;
  long lCurrentProfileTypes = 0;
  WCHAR rgwszDescription [256];

  try
  {
    // Retrieve the active policy
    NetFwPublicTypeLib::INetFwRulePtr sipFwRule;
    NetFwPublicTypeLib::INetFwPolicy2Ptr
sipFwPolicy2AsAdmin;

    CHECK_COM2(_CoCreateInstanceAsAdmin(
      GetDesktopWindow(),
      __uuidof(NetFwPolicy2),
      IID_PPV_ARGS(&sipFwPolicy2AsAdmin)));
    lCurrentProfileTypes         =         sipFwPolicy2AsAdmin-
>CurrentProfileTypes;

    // Create a new rule
    CHECK_COM2(sipFwRule.CreateInstance("HNetCfg.FwRule"));

    // Build and set the rule description string
    CHECK_COM2(StringCbPrintf(
      rgwszDescription,
      sizeof(rgwszDescription),
      L"Allow network traffic for %s",
      wszServerAppName));
    sipFwRule->Description = rgwszDescription;
```

```
    // Set the remaining rule properties
    sipFwRule->Name = wszServerAppName;
    sipFwRule->ApplicationName = wszServerAppFullPath;
    sipFwRule->Protocol = fwIpProtocol;
    sipFwRule->LocalPorts = wszLocalPort;
    sipFwRule->RemoteAddresses = wszRemoteAddresses;
    sipFwRule->Grouping = wszFirewallGrouping;
    sipFwRule->Profiles = lCurrentProfileTypes;
    sipFwRule->Action                                    =
NetFwPublicTypeLib::NET_FW_ACTION_ALLOW;
    sipFwRule->Enabled = VARIANT_TRUE;

    // Add the new rule to the active policy (effective
immediately)
    CHECK_COM2(sipFwPolicy2AsAdmin->Rules->Add(sipFwRule));
  }
  catch(_com_error& e)
  {
    hr = e.Error();
  }

  return (DWORD) hr;
}
```

There are a few things to note about the preceding sample code. Firstly, for the sake of brevity, the definition of two dependencies of this function has been omitted. One is the error-checking macro CHECK_COM2, which simply prints a debug string and throws an exception if the wrapped COM call fails. The other is the helper routine _CoCreateInstanceAsAdmin, which is essentially the same as the routine that is documented in the SDK in the COM Elevation Moniker section. See The COM Elevation Moniker in the MSDN Library for more information (http://tinyurl.com/8krm8ww).

The next thing to note about the code is that, although it uses the Windows Firewall COM classes via Visual C++, to avoid some of the usual interoperability nastiness (for example, explicitly converting LPWSTRs to BSTRs), it uses the "netfw.tlb" interop library that is included with the SDK.

The main purpose of the routine is to add the firewall rule for your demo server application. The following table lists an explanation of each property.

Property	Description
Description	A diagnostic field, visible programmatically and via the Windows Firewall with Advanced Security MMC snap-in.
Name	Take another look at Figure 2. Notice that the default firewall behavior is to use the program binary, without the extension (.exe), as its rule name. The caller of the WFAddRule function is expected to provide that string (in this case, "stcpserver") as the first parameter.
ApplicationName	This property should be set to the full path of the server-application binary. By using this property, you're preventing a binary at any other location in the file system from listening on your port.
Protocol	See the **NET_FW_IP_PROTOCOL** enumerated type in the public icftypes.h header. Defined values correspond to TCP, UDP, and ANY. This example uses this property to restrict allowed traffic to TCP.
LocalPorts	Specifies the port upon which your application is allowed to listen. For handling more complex scenarios, a comma-delimited list of ports may be used instead. See LocalPorts Property of INetFwRule in the MSDN Library for more information (http://tinyurl.com/9vbycrq).
RemoteAddresses	During testing, you will typically use this property to specify a single address on your test LAN, in order to ensure that the test client is allowed or blocked as appropriate. For deployment, more sophisticated use of this property will be required; it can take a variety of interesting values. See RemoteAddresses Property of INetFwRule in the MSDN Library for more information (http://tinyurl.com/9qgeoyr).
Grouping	This property should be used to specify a common group name for all rules that apply to a given application or feature. This demonstration requires only a single

	rule, so that the value of this property is diminished. However, its presence allows an administrator to enable, disable, and remove rules by using group name, instead of having to do this for each individually. The syntax of this property allows the value to be retrieved by using a resource table, which facilitates localization. The sample code demonstrates this "indirect string" configuration. A difficult-to-diagnose error (INetFwRules.Add returns 0x80004005) occurs if the indirect string is incorrectly configured; keep in mind that it must be loaded from system32.
Profiles	This property indicates the policy profile(s) in which the rule should apply. For the list of possible values, see the NET_FW_PROFILE_TYPE2 enumerated type in icftypes.h. Note the behavior of this test program, which installs this rule; it specifies that the new rule should apply in whichever profiles are in effect at the time of installation. However, if the server needs to be able to run under a different profile (for example, Domain versus Public), this logic will need to be modified accordingly.
Action	A given rule either blocks traffic or allows it. This example does the latter.
Enabled	A rule can be present, but disabled. However, for this solution, you want your rule to be enabled immediately; therefore, this property is set to True.

As soon as the rule is in effect, it needs to be tested. This presents a more interesting challenge, and it is the topic of the next section.

Testing

Installing the Firewall Rule and Running the Demo

As mentioned in the discussion about the WFAddRule function, that code is part of the FwTool.exe command-line utility that accompanies this chapter. The utility has three modes of operation, as displayed in its console "usage" output:

```
>FwTool.exe
Usage:
 FwTool.exe    ADD    -n    <ServerAppName>    -p    <Port>    -a
<ClientAddressRange>
 FwTool.exe DELETE -n <ServerAppName>
 FwTool.exe SHOW -n <ServerAppName>
```

In other words, the first option allows the firewall rule (as discussed in the previous section) to be created based on the specified server-application name, server port, and allowed client-address range. The second option allows the rule to be deleted. The third option displays the resulting Windows Filtering Platform filters that are created by the firewall under the covers.

To configure the server-side of the test, copy both stcpserver.exe and fwtool.exe to the system32 directory (in the sample filter output in the next section, both programs were running from a directory called "test" at the root of the volume). Then, add a rule for stcpserver in the firewall by using FwTool. For example, the following command will allow only the client at a specific IP address to connect:

```
>FwTool.exe ADD -n stcpserver -p 27015 -a 192.168.1.192

Success
```

Run stcpserver.exe on the server-side host machine, as shown in the following command. Because its rule has already been added to the firewall, you shouldn't see a Windows Security Alert dialog box.

```
>stcpserver.exe

Listening on socket bound to 0.0.0.0:27015 ...
```

Run stcpclient on the client-side host machine, as shown in the following command. The server DNS name must be specified on the command-line. Because this client is the one that is allowed by the installed firewall rule, it immediately connects, exchanges some data with the server, and disconnects.

```
>stcpclient.exe testmachine6
Secure connection established to the server
Sent 8 bytes of data to the server
Received 11 bytes of data from the server
Finished
```

Here's the additional output that is displayed by the server in response to the client-connect and data-exchange. Then, the server re-listens on its socket.

```
>stcpserver.exe
Listening on socket bound to 0.0.0.0:27015 ...
Connected to a client
Received 8 bytes of data from the client
Sent 11 bytes of data to the client
Listening on socket bound to 0.0.0.0:27015 ...
```

Displaying the Resulting Filters

```
>FwTool.exe SHOW -n stcpserver
Filter Name: stcpserver, Action: 0x1002, Effective Weight: 0xd92fd4
 SubLayer: Windows Firewall, Weight: 2
Match Field: IP_LOCAL_PORT, Type: 0, Value: 27015
Match Field: APP_ID, Type: 0, Value:
0000    5c 00 64 00 65 00 76 00 69 00 63 00 65 00 5c 00
\.d.e.v.i.c.e.\.
0010    68 00 61 00 72 00 64 00 64 00 69 00 73 00 6b 00
h.a.r.d.d.i.s.k.
0020    76 00 6f 00 6c 00 75 00 6d 00 65 00 34 00 5c 00
v.o.l.u.m.e.4.\.
0030    74 00 65 00 73 00 74 00 5c 00 73 00 74 00 63 00
t.e.s.t.\.s.t.c.
0040    70 00 73 00 65 00 72 00 76 00 65 00 72 00 2e 00
p.s.e.r.v.e.r...
0050  65 00 78 00 65 00 00 00                 e.x.e...

Filter Name: stcpserver, Action: 0x1002, Effective Weight: 0xd96f8c
 SubLayer: Windows Firewall, Weight: 2
Match Field: IP_LOCAL_PORT, Type: 0, Value: 27015
Match Field: APP_ID, Type: 0, Value:
0000    5c 00 64 00 65 00 76 00 69 00 63 00 65 00 5c 00
\.d.e.v.i.c.e.\.
0010    68 00 61 00 72 00 64 00 64 00 69 00 73 00 6b 00
h.a.r.d.d.i.s.k.
0020    76 00 6f 00 6c 00 75 00 6d 00 65 00 34 00 5c 00
v.o.l.u.m.e.4.\.
0030    74 00 65 00 73 00 74 00 5c 00 73 00 74 00 63 00
t.e.s.t.\.s.t.c.
0040    70 00 73 00 65 00 72 00 76 00 65 00 72 00 2e 00
p.s.e.r.v.e.r...
0050  65 00 78 00 65 00 00 00                 e.x.e...
Match Field: IP_REMOTE_ADDRESS, Type: 0, Value:
 Addr = 192.168.1.192
 Mask = 0.0.0.0
Match Field: IP_PROTOCOL, Type: 0, Value: 6
Success
```

The Windows Firewall with Advanced Security MMC Snap-In

Windows includes a built-in firewall-management console, which (along with FwTool.exe) is a useful way to check your work as you are developing and testing the rule code that is discussed in the previous section.

To access the console, click **Start**, type **WF.msc**, and then press **Enter**. You can start by selecting **Inbound Rules** in the left pane. It's educational to examine the rules that are present by default.

After you add the custom rule by using FwTool, as described earlier, select **Filter by Group** in the Actions pane on the right. Sure enough, one of the listed options is the TCP Server demo group that is created by this code, as shown in Figure 3.

Figure 3 TCP Server demo-group option in Windows Vista

In the center pane of Figure 3, all of the expected properties of the custom rule are present (including a number of fields that are not showing, as the image would have been too wide). For example, the host machine is a member of a test (Active Directory) domain, and was on that network (that is, as opposed to a roaming laptop that is connected to public Wi-Fi) at the time that the rule was added. Therefore, the rule is applied in the Domain profile. Also, note that a single test client is configured to be allowed through the filter—namely, the client with IPv4 address 192.168.1.192.

Comparing the Custom Rule to the Default

During the course of developing this custom firewall rule for the stcspserver.exe test application, you can use the FwTool.exe "show" option to sanity-check your work. It's also interesting to use that tool to compare the custom rule to the rule that's created by default. Note that the default rule is created in the following situation:

1. No previous firewall rule exists for an application.

2. That application attempts to open a network port.

3. The Windows Security Alert dialog box appears (see Figure 4).

4. The user clicks the Unblock button (or the Keep blocking button, which results in a different set of default rules).

It is recommended that you use the sample application to cause the default Unblock rules to be created and to use the firewall MMC snap-in to review them. Not surprisingly, when this happens, all network traffic on any port and from any client can now be received by the designated application. This is perhaps a reasonable default behavior (based on the assumption that the user recognizes the application in question as trustworthy), given the need to compromise between usability and security in a consumer operating system. However, it further reinforces why the application developer should implement a much tighter rule configuration for installation (and for un-installation).

Testing Each Rule Property

As soon as the stcpserver.exe application rule is configured, you'll want to test each property of it, to ensure that you are demonstrating a truly locked-down configuration. With that said, some of the properties are easier to test than others. Furthermore, there are some properties that you'll likely want to test on an as-needed basis—and testing these would require modifying the socket-related code on the client, as well as on the server. However, you don't want to expose this in the command-line options (for example, the ability to send and receive UDP traffic). To avoid that extra work, you can use an existing network-testing tool called NetCat (http://tinyurl.com/cfezlb).

Application Name

First, as a warm-up for the testing phase of preparing this demo, you want to ensure that, based on your new firewall rule, only the designated server-application name is allowed to listen on the open port. Start by configuring the server rule as discussed earlier.

```
>FwTool.exe add -n stcpserver -p 27015 -a 192.168.1.192
Success
```

Next, run NetCat (nc.exe) on the same server, with the appropriate command-line options to listen on the same port (type **nc.exe –h** for command-line help).

```
>nc.exe -l -p 27015
```

As a result, you immediately see the Windows Security Alert dialog box.

Figure 4 Windows Security Alert dialog box in Windows Vista

This is good; it indicates that, even though there are conditional "unblock" rules associated with the server-application port, only binaries of the same name can open it. However, it's important to mention that even a totally different application, if renamed to "stcpserver.exe," can indeed open the port.

```
>del stcpserver.exe
>ren nc.exe stcpserver.exe
>stcpserver.exe -l -p 27015
```

Next, run the client application (shown in the following code block) from an allowed machine. In response, you will see "12345678" displayed by stcpserver/nc.exe on the server, indicating that the connection and data transmission were successful.

```
>stcpclient.exe testmachine6
Secure connection established to the server
Sent 8 bytes of data to the server
```

Therefore, it is indeed possible to bend the firewall rules a little more than you might like! Of course, if an attacker is actually able to run code in this manner on a server, there may be broader security problems to worry about.

One final note about testing: you want to be sure to remove any firewall rules that were created by each test scenario, in order to ensure that downstream test results won't be affected. This can be accomplished via FwTool.exe tool (shown in the following code) or the firewall MMC snap-in (see previous). Also, after running this particular test case, don't forget to rename nc.exe and stcpserver.exe, as appropriate!

```
>FwTool.exe delete -n nc
Success
>FwTool.exe delete -n stcpserver
Success
```

Protocol

In addition to verifying the behavior of the application-identity filter that you added, you'll want to confirm that the protocol filter is working as expected. In particular, only TCP traffic should be traversing the firewall, based on the rule: no UDP traffic. This is easily confirmed by using a variation of the test configuration that is discussed in the previous section.

First, add a rule to allow NetCat the same network access that you granted the stcpserver demo application.

```
>FwTool.exe add -n nc -p 27015 -a 192.168.1.192
Success
```

During any testing effort, it's recommended that you run a "positive" test case in conjunction with every "negative" test case. In other words, try the variation that should work, and then change a single variable to try the variation that shouldn't work. This pattern is especially important when testing something as complex—and as critically important—as network security. To accomplish this in the current test scenario, you can run NetCat in TCP listen mode (its default) on the server as a positive test case.

```
>nc.exe -l -p 27015
```

Running NetCat in connect mode from the client confirms that the rule is allowing TCP traffic through.

```
>nc.exe testmachine6 27015
adsfasdfasdfasdf
```

How do you know that traffic is passing through the firewall? The "adsfasdfasdfasdf" string is echoed on the server (not shown). Finally, re-run the preceding two commands, but include the NetCat command-line option to send (and listen for) UDP packets instead of TCP. On the server:

```
>nc.exe -l -p 27015 -u
```

Then, run the corresponding client-connect command:

```
>nc -u jwsecure-v6 27015
asdfasdfasdfasdf
```

Confirm that the text that you entered at the client was not echoed on the server. Finally, clean up the created rules on the server to prepare for the next phase of testing.

```
>FwTool.exe delete -n nc
Success
>FwTool.exe delete -n stcpserver
Success
```

Client Address

Verifying the client-address component of the demo rule is also straightforward. The optimal test scenario for the client-address filter requires three machines: a server, an allowed client, and a denied client. However, there are also a variety of permutations that don't require a second client.

The first step is to set up the server rule and confirm that the allowed client can successfully connect, as discussed previously at the beginning of the Testing section. Then, attempt to connect to the server from a different client (that is, a different IP address).

```
>stcpclient.exe jwsecure-v6
WSAConnect returned error 10060
SecureTcpConnect returned error 10060
```

The preceding error code corresponds to "Connection timed out." See Windows Sockets Error Codes in the MSDN Library for more information (http://tinyurl.com/6xqbtu). This confirms the negative test case, as expected: a disallowed client address cannot connect to the server.

ENDPOINT RESILIENCY

13 REDUCING ATTACKS

"A secure desktop environment starts with a holistic approach to reduce the attack surface and enables devices to continue performing while under attack. Learn how to create the foundation that can evolve with your networks."

-Secure Approach, Microsoft TechNet

Quality of Service

Intel has introduced a quality of service-like extension called the Intel CPU Web API (http://tinyurl.com/9ecfxr8). In addition to monitoring devices for their security disposition, and exposing that data to applications, it allows you to check for other information, such as the remaining battery life on a laptop. For example, a digital media website could use this information to warn a user watching a movie that her laptop is going to run out of power before the film is complete, allowing her to plug-in before that happens.

Of course, a network security manager in an enterprise environment may not want certain information about the organization's endpoint devices to be exposed outside of the network—this information could, potentially, be used to inform adversaries of weaknesses in an organization's defenses. It's one thing for an external website to check the battery life of a laptop; it's another thing for that website to be able to determine the Active Directory group membership of a corporate executive who happens to be watching a movie online.

Thus, the second pillar in the Four Pillars of Endpoint Security—Endpoint Resiliency—isn't just about exposing device health information to the cloud; it's also about controlling how that information is used, and by whom.

Data Loss Prevention

Realistically, a defense-in-depth approach is the correct strategy: strong authentication, granular authorization, rights management, filtering at the perimeter, plus auditing. The space is wide open right now, though. Major software vendors such as Symantec and Microsoft have partial solutions in place, but the biggest gap is integration: finding service providers who understand the threats, what's available, what's not, and how to bridge the gaps.

In an age of smartphones and tablets, users have become accustomed to anytime/anywhere data access. This puts IT professionals between a rock and a hard place. So, how can you implement nuanced compliance rules, provide data loss prevention, and at the same time allow quick and easy data access anytime, anywhere, to authorized users? That is the goal of Dynamic Access Control in Windows 8.

In short, Dynamic Access Control is designed to make existing authorization tools more expressive. The most common form of access control management today is the security group. In a role-based access control model using security groups, a group will be created for a collection of data. When a user assumes a role that requires access to the data, the user is made a member of the security group for as long as access is needed. This first level of authorization abstraction interposes the role (or group identity) between the user and the data. But with ever increasing complexity of compliance mandates, the number of security groups has proliferated to the point where a large enterprise user may need to belong to tens to hundreds of groups to accommodate fine-grained control.

An additional complication is the growing number of geographical compliance mandates designed to keep sensitive personal data inside a country's borders. These mandates are intended to ensure that data transit does not result in relaxation of compliance rules, and are a well-known compliance implementation hurdle in the European Union.

The only place where data access can be effectively controlled is at the server where the data resides. But the tradeoff is loss of centralized control of policy. In response to this dichotomy, Dynamic Access Control has been designed to provide solid access control at this most appropriate location while maintaining a central control store for authorization information.

From a business perspective, two primary reasons for centralized control are proof of compliance and ease of management. To meet the first requirement, use a strategy of creating labels to enable the compliance rules to determine if the data needs to be controlled. To meet the second, create central policy based on the compliance category.

With current technologies, such as the discretionary access control list (DACL, or just ACL) feature in file systems like NTFS, IT security engineers have long recognized that some compliance rules do not fit the usual user/group attributes. Regulations prevent data from leaving a political or geographic region, or mandate that the devices that access the data will not inadvertently leak it from the control boundary. These attributes become accessible with Dynamic Access Control—the location and health of the device can be included in the claims delivered to the server that performs the access check together with the policies that need to be enforced.

The following websites describe more about the new capabilities of Dynamic Access Control in Windows 8 and how you can benefit from it:

- Dynamic Access Control: Scenario Overview (http://tinyurl.com/ct8suqm)

- How to use central access policies for dynamic access control (http://tinyurl.com/bqs4czs)

NETWORK RESILIENCY

14 TRUSTED BOOT

An easy way to prioritize the use of network resources is to ensure that only authorized, secure devices have access. This section discusses how Trusted Platform Module (TPM), trusted boot, and platform attestation can be used to provide high-assurance endpoint device authorization.

In the James Bond film, *Casino Royale*, a high-stakes poker game is arranged as a gambit to lure a desperate terrorist to the table. Before the game begins, each player types in a secure PIN on a mobile banking kiosk, which is essentially a laptop with a special number pad. The PIN will later be used to authorize a funds transfer if that player wins the game. Of course, James Bond wins the poker game. When the Swiss banker returns with the mobile kiosk to complete the funds transfer, Bond invites his new girlfriend to type in his PIN. "How could I know it?" she asks. Well, it turns out that the PIN code he used is actually her name. Cue the cheesy romantic montage.

And yet, while the context is as hackneyed as one might expect from James Bond, the Swiss banker's mobile kiosk presents particularly interesting questions about endpoint security. After all, mobile banking is becoming the norm. If hackers had been able to perform a brute-force guessing attack on Bond's PIN, they would have found it quickly. Therefore, the bank doesn't want just anybody to be able to access its private funds transfer system, even though that system needs to be accessible to a mobile device that could be operating anywhere.

In addition to the dubious integrity of Bond's PIN, it's necessary to consider the security of the mobile kiosk itself. It's possible that hackers or a trusted insider could compromise the device by installing a keystroke logger or other malware. With access to such a highly trusted device, hackers could wreak havoc, liquidating customer accounts at their leisure. What can the banking industry do to secure mobile devices against such threats?

Trusted Boot

A compelling solution for securing the mobile banking scenario depicted in *Casino Royale* is trusted boot with remote attestation. The Trusted Platform Module (TPM) is a tamper-resistant security chip installed on many PCs. The TPM works with the computer BIOS to monitor what happens as the computer starts up. During the boot process, the TPM records data, or *measurements*, such as the identity of the operating system loader and other binaries. Once the PC has started up, the data gathered by the TPM is available to be queried. The TPM applies a digital signature to the boot data in order to guarantee its integrity.

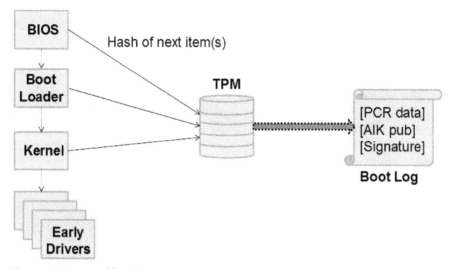

Figure 5 Measured boot

The information that the TPM gathers about the boot sequence is critical in the mobile banking kiosk scenario since it allows a chain of trust, starting from the PC hardware and extending to the operating system and user apps, to be established. If a hacker modifies any of the components in that chain, it's critical to know about it. Likewise, if a hacker adds any untrusted components to the chain, it's critical to know about those as well.

Antivirus

It's one thing to gather the boot data from the TPM, list the loader and boot drivers that are present, and even to verify the digital signature of those binaries. However, it's quite another thing to determine whether those binaries—even if they're signed—are actually the correct ones. This verification is the role the antivirus solutions have long played: if an attempt is made to run a program or open a file that is recognized to include something bad or untrusted, then the antivirus solution blocks it.

In order for a trusted boot solution to be practical, the same antivirus procedure needs to be done when the PC is starting up. As early as possible during the boot sequence, an antivirus driver should load and monitor all of the binaries loaded thereafter. The antivirus driver complements the TPM. While the TPM is taking measurements that can later be verified cryptographically, the antivirus driver is looking for risky files in real time. In order to ensure that only trusted components are loaded, one of the measurements that the TPM takes is the identity of the antivirus driver itself. This measurement ensures that only the trusted, un-tampered antivirus software is loaded.

Remote Attestation

The OEM, or the organization that purchased the PC, can preconfigure the TPM with a secret key. The TPM can also use a key to digitally sign the boot data (also known as a boot log) gathered during startup. Referring back to the chain of trust mentioned earlier, the TPM key is the first link in that chain and the antivirus driver is the last. If you can verify with high assurance that each link in the chain is a trusted binary, and if you trust that your antivirus solution will protect the PC once it's running, then all that remains to verify the machine's integrity is to be able to demonstrate to a remote server that the chain of trust is intact. This validation is accomplished by using a process called *remote attestation*.

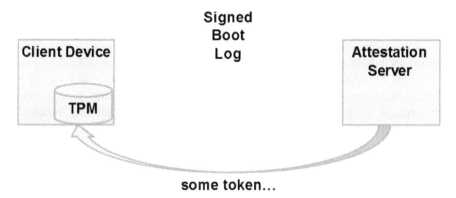

Figure 6 Remote attestation

During the process of remote attestation, the TPM boot data is gathered, signed with a trusted key, and is then sent to a remote server for verification. In the mobile banking scenario, the software running on the kiosk laptop would perform remote attestation as part of authenticating to the funds transfer system. Before allowing the transaction, the funds transfer system verifies the following components:

- Integrity of the signed boot log received from the client/kiosk

- Identity of the TPM key

- Presence of a trusted boot loader, antivirus driver, and any other binaries loaded before or between these components

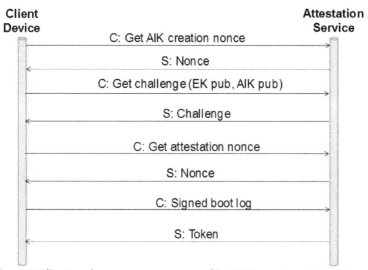

Figure 7 Client and server messages used in TPM remote attestation

Finally, a Plot Twist

If you've seen *Casino Royale*, you know that James Bond's winnings were in fact diverted, but not because of a compromised device. Instead, it was a trusted insider. Indeed, there's little that can be done to prevent an attack by someone who misuses his or her explicitly granted privileged access.

Rather, the best strategy for mitigating the threat of a trusted insider misusing his or her access is to audit those transactions. Trusted boot is useful here since it allows you to track who did what, what device that person used to perform the action, and when the action was committed, with high assurance.

The TPM key allows a specific device to be registered to a specific user. Combining remote attestation with some form of user authentication allows a user/machine binding to be enforced. If a trusted user attempts a transaction from the wrong kiosk, that action should be flagged as a potential stolen credential. Likewise, if an untrusted user attempts a transaction from a trusted kiosk, that action should be flagged as an indication that the kiosk might have been stolen.

15 MORE ON MEASURED BOOT

One of the notable areas of innovation in Windows 8 is building on the Trusted Platform Module (TPM), which is a tamper-resistant security chip that has been built into many PC motherboards for the past several years (or, more recently, integrated as firmware into system-on-a-chip architectures). Of the TPM-related features, one interesting feature is measured boot. It's introduced in this video from BUILD (http://tinyurl.com/9fkpcx4). In short, it computes a cryptographic hash of the operating system boot loader and boot drivers. This is critical for blocking malware such as rootkits, which load early in the boot cycle in order to effectively become invisible to antivirus software which loads much later.

If you install the Win 8 developer preview build on a TPM-capable machine (e.g. a 64-bit HP ProBook 6360b), measured boot is turned on by default. You'll need a third-party tool to view the data, or you can build your own from an SDK sample Microsoft has provided.

Once the cryptographic loader and driver hashes have been computed, and the system is booted, a log file that lists those hashes can be generated. This is where things get interesting. The hash of the boot loader is protected by the TPM itself. Further, the TPM can be provisioned with a cryptographic key, which can be used to sign a measured boot-log file. Thus, if you trust the TPM key, and you trust that a user can't muck with the TPM itself (generally considered to be very hard, but not impossible), then you can establish a hardware-rooted trust chain for all of the drivers in the log file.

Measured boot has limitations. For one thing, it only protects early-boot drivers (including an optional Early-Load Anti-Malware [ELAM] driver, which is expected to be provided by antivirus vendors—see the Secured Boot Architecture slide in the BUILD presentation). For software higher in the stack, including most device drivers and anything loaded in user mode (e.g. browser plug-ins), you're trusting your antivirus software to protect you. Second, the measurement part of measured boot only happens at boot time (see the TPM Basics slide in the BUILD presentation). After that, until the next reboot, you're trusting your antivirus software to do its job.

The ELAM/anti-malware opportunity is intriguing, but where measured boot really shines is in the context of remote attestation. Remote attestation is just a fancy, albeit descriptive, name for the process of taking the signed log file described above and sending it off-box for verification. The ramifications of that ability may not be immediately obvious, but they're significant, since the main weak point of authentication schemes today is, "How do we really know that the client PC is acting on behalf of the user?"

In current authentication schemes, a server has no way of knowing whether a rootkit has been installed on a remote client. Compromised client computers are more likely to be used in fraudulent transactions. With remote attestation, a trusted TPM, and a trusted anti-malware/ELAM solution in place, the server can authorize the user to perform high-value transactions with higher assurance (e.g. transfer money or get a driver's license).

To see measured boot in action, download and run the Platform Crypto Provider test from the Windows Hardware Compatibility Kit (http://tinyurl.com/cd58mq9). The pcptool.exe test binary offers a command-line interface for interacting not only with measured boot, but also with other TPM-related features discussed in the BUILD presentation.

With pcptool.exe, you can retrieve the binary version of the measured boot log data as follows:

```
>PCPTool.exe GetLog c:\temp\bootlog.out
```

Then, to convert the binary into XML:

```
>PCPTool.exe    DecodeLog    c:\temp\bootlog.out    >
c:\temp\bootlog-decoded.txt
```

Finally, it's instructive to examine the contents of the XML log file:

```
<LoadedModule_Aggregation                        Size="435">
  <FilePath
Size="60">\Windows\system32\winload.exe</FilePath>
  <ImageSize    Size="8">1286144<!-    0x000000000013a000 -
></ImageSize>
  <HashAlgorithmId    Size="4">SHA-256</HashAlgorithmId>
  <AuthenticodeHash                               Size="32">

9cb15db889bb78400e4cc6831d04616c013bf904b097cedb503e5136e575
0b16
  </AuthenticodeHash>
…         <AuthoritySHA1Thumbprint            Size="20">
    cc9008d2d4e80eb924e3ad29cb08600f58570cdc
    <!-              …………….XW..                       ->
  </AuthoritySHA1Thumbprint>
</LoadedModule_Aggregation>
```

The above log entry shows the hash and signer information for the Windows boot loader. Again, combined with remote attestation, this information can be evaluated by a remote server to establish cryptographically that early system boot components have not been modified.

16 SECURING RESOURCES

In the last five years, the number of cloud services has increased considerably. With this increase, users are becoming more accustomed to conducting business on the Internet. The integrity of these types of services requires that both users' computers and the servers hosting the users' data are healthy and secure.

A New Model for Distributed System Health

At the 2011 RSA Conference, Scott Charney, Vice President of Trustworthy Computing at Microsoft, stated that computer security on the Internet is "in somewhat of a state of paralysis." He proposed a new way of thinking about security, likening it to the public health system. Charney noted that world health organizations are getting quite good at identifying and eliminating threats to public health. As people have become more mobile, so have disease carriers, and the same change is coming to our computing systems.

Originally, computing systems were in a single location and external data transfer was difficult. However, we now expect to have instant access to all data through a variety of devices, including full featured applications on a smartphone that we carry in a pocket. In the early days of mobile computing, traveling business people had to initiate a secure connection to the enterprise network so that the remote computer could be treated as though it were operating inside of the enterprise perimeter, protected by the enterprise firewall, in order to access any corporate data. Now users expect to be able to work anywhere, at any time, and on any device.

Current State of the Network Perimeter

The traditional enterprise security perimeter is being further eroded by cloud computing. In a traditional enterprise domain, all computer services ran on the enterprise network and could rely on Active Directory Domain Services (AD DS) for authentication of users and machines, authorization of access requests, and management of configuration. Each user was authenticated by AD DS, each computer was managed, and servers were on the premises inside a firewall-protected network perimeter.

As the workforce has become more mobile, and IT falls under increasing pressure to cut costs, organizations have been moving toward supporting employee-owned equipment and for customers to access services from any computer that is attached to the Internet. These changes have driven the creation of richer and more mobile-capable experiences, but have come with challenges. The processes for managing services have had to change as much of the network topography has moved into the cloud and outside of the network perimeter. Managing access control for managed and unmanaged computers in this new environment can be difficult. Authentication and authorization increase in complexity, relying on technologies such as federation, as well as new web-based configuration interfaces exposed by cloud service providers. In addition, unmanaged client computers are more likely to be infected with malware. These uncertainties complicate compliance, and further weaken the security perimeter of the hosted service that the infected computer is accessing.

Locking Down Computers: Don't Discard Your Tools

In addition to compromising the stability of internal systems and enterprise data, infected computers can cause customer data and credentials to be leaked. However, as we become more dependent on cloud services, it's important that we not forget about our usual security tools—they're still useful!

For example, the health of domain-joined computers can be managed by controlling the code that is installed on them. Since the release of User Account Control (UAC) with Windows Vista, fewer applications are granted administrative privileges, ensuring that malware does not get control of many domain-joined computers today. Another example of a feature that can be used for controlling the code that can run on Windows is AppLocker, a security feature that allows IT admins to control which executables are permitted to run by policy (http://tinyurl.com/9jp2qw4). While features such as AppLocker are best configured and managed using Active Directory, and cloud scenarios do tend to involve some computers and services that are outside the reach of Active Directory, most medium-sized and larger organizations will continue to use Active Directory to manage client computers, on-premise servers, and Infrastructure as a Service (IaaS) hosted servers for the foreseeable future.

Another example of a still-useful security technology for the cloud is Network Access Protection (NAP), also known in the industry as Network Access Control (NAC) (http://tinyurl.com/9h56t9a). With NAP, when determining the health level of an internal computer, an organization can measure and enforce the client computer's level of access. As discussed earlier, NAP is another AD-dependent technology, but it still applies in the

71

off-premise and IaaS scenarios. Indeed, with increasing exposure of enterprise computing resources to the outside world, the NAP quarantine capability is important for keeping malware off the network, and for keeping sensitive data secure.

To digress briefly, the NAP/NAC model is one that can and should be revisited by the major technology vendors and made more cloud-friendly. For example, by extending the NAP client components to issue SAML-compatible health claims, a whole range of federation scenarios, including authentication to cloud services, could be enhanced with client quarantine and remediation capabilities. This extension is particularly important since many customers are finding that cloud services lack the rich set of authorization controls exposed by on-premise applications that integrate with Active Directory. By mating NAP with health claims, more granular access control of cloud services is afforded based on explicit assertions from the client. Extending Scott Charney's public health analogy further, we see claims-based NAP being complemented by a hosted service, which tracks the health history of a computer. This would be useful for estimating the fraud risk of a given transaction, for example.

Returning to the discussion about existing tools, there are plenty of other security technologies to consider in the context of cloud computing.

- As a showcase of the state of the art, the NSA has created a High Assurance Platform (HAP) effort to provide security configuration guidance to all organizations on the methods to protect their computers from remote attack (http://tinyurl.com/8zqg4a3).

- For recent versions of the Windows operating system, Microsoft offers the Microsoft Security Compliance Manager (SCM), which allows IT professionals to access and automate all of an organization's security configuration baselines in a centralized location. These baselines can then be applied to individual computers by using Group Policy, Microsoft System Center Configuration Manager (SCCM), or by using a Security Content Automation Protocol (SCAP) scanner that meets National Institute of Standards and Technology (NIST) specifications.

- The Center for Internet Security (CIS) has a download center for secure configuration benchmarks, including one for Windows 7 (http://tinyurl.com/6obacfj).

When exploring the adoption of cloud services, a pain-point commonly expressed by customers today is a perceived loss of control. In the current cloud services landscape, it is believed that loss of control is more than just perception—it's real, and it represents an opportunity for technology providers to provide richer capabilities for customer configuration of their offerings. A good example of a rich configuration capability is fine-grained control of authorization rules. Client health claims and health history should play a role in that capability.

However, IT administrators must not abandon their existing skills and tools. Indeed, for the all the hype about how cloud services will cost IT professionals their jobs, it's possible that the opposite is true: while IT jobs will almost certainly shift, there will be a net gain in demand, since securing the enterprise is getting harder every day, not easier. And while most cloud services available now are new offerings, the same techniques will apply when locking them down.

NETWORK PRIORITIZATION

17 NETWORK ACCESS PROTECTION

Network Access Protection (NAP) is a feature that helps to protect network resources from insecure computers. Although NAP is a complex and extensible technology, it's easy to gain a basic understanding of it by considering a common deployment scenario.

NETWORK ACCESS PROTECTION

Suppose that an enterprise called Contoso has deployed a Remote Access server (RAS) to allow traveling employees to access the corporate network from the road. While RAS access is critical for the productivity of Contoso's employees, and the underlying protocols that are used by RAS provide robust authentication and encryption, exposing the corporate network to roaming computers nevertheless increases its attack surface. For example, roaming computers are frequently exposed to high-risk hotel and coffee-shop wireless networks. Such machines, therefore, have higher malicious-software (malware) and virus exposure.

To help combat the security risk that is introduced by allowing roaming computers to connect, Contoso's network administrators ensure that roaming machines are as healthy as possible before allowing them to connect (e.g. they want to confirm that every client has installed the latest patches from Microsoft Update). Network administrators accomplish this by enabling NAP on the RAS server and on the RAS/VPN clients. In fact, NAP has built-in support for verifying that clients have the latest Microsoft security updates.

With NAP enabled in the RAS scenario, clients who attempt to connect must pass the health check that is administered by the RAS server. If the health check succeeds (that is, the NAP client reports that the latest security patches have been installed), the virtual private network (VPN) connection is established. If the health check fails, NAP allows clients to automatically attempt to correct the problem (that is, to download and install the latest security patches, in this case) and to reattempt the RAS connection. If the health problem is not corrected, the client is not allowed to connect, thus keeping unpatched systems off of the corporate network.

With that scenario in mind, consider that NAP is actually more broadly applicable. For one thing, RAS/VPN isn't the only NAP-enabled network service. The other NAP-enabled network services in Microsoft Windows Server 2008 include DHCP, IPsec, and 802.1X.

Also broadening NAP's applicability is the fact that the health-check architecture supports a plug-in model. This is demonstrated in the sample code in Chapter 12, Hardening with the Firewall.

Network Access Protection

This sample solution builds upon the deployment scenario introduced earlier. In this example, suppose that you're a programmer for a line-of-business (LOB) application-development team at a large enterprise. The company, Contoso, has a large sales department, and many of those employees spend a lot of time on the road. As a result, Contoso is heavily dependent upon its remote-access infrastructure, which allows its sales team to access data and applications reliably on the corporate network while they travel.

The nature of this environment is such that many of Contoso's employees are accessing corpnet resources from networks with high-risk profiles. For example, hotel and coffee-shop networks are not known to be the most secure, especially when compared to Contoso's. The workstations that are used by Contoso's traveling sales force face heavy virus and malware exposure.

Furthermore, Contoso's administrators recognize that as connectivity needs increase, enterprise network perimeters are becoming more permeable. For example, the machines (laptops, typically) that are used by traveling employees are at times docked, or connected directly to the corporate network behind the firewall. Thus, the VPN servers aren't the only point of entry for high-risk clients; on-site services such as DHCP also are at risk.

Therefore, Contoso's system administrators are deploying Network Access Protection (NAP) in order to better protect corporate resources from these potentially unhealthy client machines. NAP is available across multiple scenarios, including VPN and DHCP. In addition, NAP's extensibility allows the sysadmins to determine which client health policies to enforce, and when to modify those policies over time.

However, while NAP is indeed extensible, doing so generally involves implementing certain COM plug-in interfaces via Visual C++ code. This is not an area in which the average sysadmin is particularly strong! This creates a dependency on you and the rest of Contoso's LOB dev team to respond to the sysadmins in a timely manner, each time a new health policy is required for enforcement, or each time a significant change to an existing policy plug-in is required. The relative complexity of most COM/Visual C++ interfaces, as well as the increased testing burden, is such that this dependency is likely to result in deployment delays that Contoso's administrators would prefer to avoid.

Fortunately for the LOB devs and the sysadmins, the observation was made that many decisions about client-workstation health are made based (either directly or indirectly) on information that is read from the Windows registry. As a result, a generic NAP solution could be created that is based simply on a list of target registry keys, as well as expected values, provided at run-time. Those clients without the expected registry settings, whatever they happen to be, will be considered unhealthy.

Solution Architecture

The system administrators and LOB programmers at Contoso have agreed upon a generic solution for NAP extensibility. By allowing a to-be-defined list of client registry keys to be checked, a broad set of configuration policies can be enforced without incurring a downstream dependency upon low-level programming skill.

This solution consists of the following pieces:

1. **Registry System Health Agent (SHA)**—The SHA interface is what exposes NAP client-side extensibility; the Registry SHA is thus a COM DLL that implements this interface. The Registry SHA implements the policy reporting that was discussed earlier (i.e. accept an arbitrary list of registry keys, and report their values).

2. **Registry SHA service**—This Microsoft Windows NT service hosts the Registry SHA on the client, registering its interface upon startup.

3. **Registry System Health Validator (SHV)**—The SHV interface is what exposes NAP server-side extensibility. Like its SHA counterpart

on the client, the Registry SHV is a COM DLL. The SHV allows the administrator to define a list of registry keys and expected values. Based on the actual values that are reported by the client SHA, the SHV determines whether the client should be considered healthy or otherwise.

Message Flow

Figure 8 shows the message flow between logical components for a typical NAP-enabled scenario—DHCP, in this case. A description of the messages and principals that are involved follows.

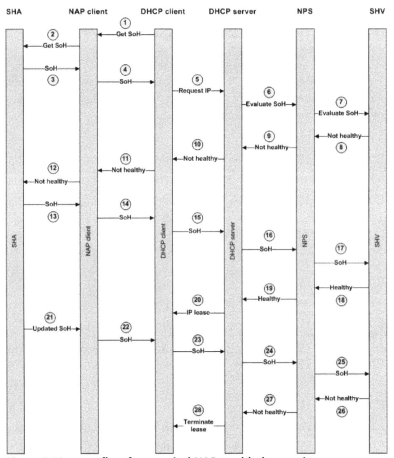

Figure 8 Message flow for a typical NAP-enabled scenario

Figure 8 illustrates the following scenario:

1. The client workstation prepares to request an IP address from the DHCP server. The DHCP client is configured with Group Policy to be NAP-enabled. As a result, it contacts the NAP client service. Note that the DHCP client, NAP client, and SHA are all components that are running on the client workstation.

2. The NAP client service requests a Statement of Health (SoH) from each registered SHA, and possibly including those provided by Microsoft, as well as any third-party plug-ins, such as the Registry SHA.

3. The SoH request is returned by each SHA and gathered by the NAP client.

4. The collective client SoH request data is returned by the NAP client to the DHCP client.

5. The workstation DHCP client makes its request for an IP address lease from the network DHCP server. The client SoH is included in this request.

6. Upon receipt of the IP lease request, the DHCP server must consult a Network Policy Server (NPS) to evaluate the client SoH. The NPS may be running on a separate server, but not necessarily.

7. For each SHA that is running on the client, a corresponding SHV is expected to be present on the NPS. Thus, NAP's extensibility consists of SHA/SHV pairs. For example, if the demo Registry SHA were installed on the client workstation, its SoH would now be passed to the Registry SHV to be evaluated.

8. In this scenario, suppose that the SoH information that is provided by the client does not meet the policy requirements that are configured on the NPS. For example, in the sample Registry SHA/SHV case, the SoH may have shown a required security-related registry key to be missing. In the not-healthy case, an SHV optionally can return remediation instructions to the client. The sample Registry SHV implements this feature, which allows the security posture of the client workstation to be corrected automatically without direct user intervention. This *auto-remediation* is an important feature of

NAP; it reduces the administrative overhead of providing client connectivity, while maintaining network security.

9. The SoH response passes back through each component in the logical chain, eventually making its way to each corresponding SHA on the client workstation.

10. If the SoH response indicates that the client is unhealthy, any of the SHAs that are configured to handle auto-remediation can now act upon the fix instructions that are provided by the SHV. Of course, in general, remediation could succeed or fail for any number of reasons. Either way, if remediation was requested, the result of that operation is returned to the NAP client, and then back to the NPS and SHV.

11. Only after the client is determined to be healthy is the request for an IP address satisfied.

12. Sometime subsequent to the completion of DHCP, the security status of the client may change. For example, in the case of the Registry SHA, a piece of client software could make a registry change to one of the keys that are being monitored. In response, the SHA prepares a new SoH request and notifies the NAP client. As an aside, there are conceivable scenarios in which it doesn't make sense for a SHA to monitor client health changes dynamically. For example, suppose that a SHA/SHV pair checks on the processor architecture of the client machine. That information is unlikely to change—at least, without a reboot.

13. In response to the updated SoH request, if the client is deemed unhealthy and remediation fails, the DHCP server terminates the client IP lease.

Architecture Diagram

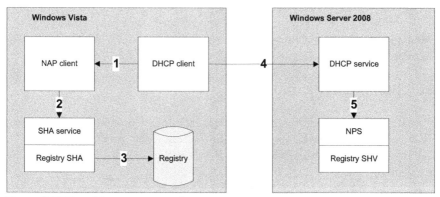

Figure 9 NAP architecture scenario

Figure 9 depicts the following scenario:

1. The Windows Vista client has been configured to use NAP-enabled DHCP. As a result, when the workstation needs to request an IP address, the DHCP client first requests a SoH from the NAP client.

2. System Health Agents are registered with NAP on the client workstation. See the sample SHA COM registration logic in sha\dll\sdkshamodule.cpp!CSdkShaModule::RegisterSdkSha in the accompanying sample code. The NAP client consults each registered SHA for its SoH. See sha\exe\callback.cpp!ShaCallback::GetSoHRequest in the sample code.

3. The sample Registry SHA queries the local registry keys and values, per its configuration. (See sha\exe\callback.cpp!ShaCallback::FillSoHRequest).

4. As soon as the NAP client has prepared a SoH, the DHCP client sends its request to the DHCP server.

5. The DHCP server sends the client SoH to the NPS. The NPS is shown on the same server as the DHCP service, but they can be separate. The NPS consults the SHV plug-ins that correspond to each SHA on the client. Based on the data that is reported by each SHA, the SHVs determine if the client is healthy or otherwise. (See shv\sampleshv.cpp!CSampleShv::CheckRequestSoHHealth in the sample code.)

For the sample server-side logic, see: shv\samplesshv.cpp!CSampleShv::FillResponseSoH. For the sample client-side logic, see sha\exe\callback.cpp!ShaCallback::ProcessSoHResponse and ::DoPatch.

Solution Implementation

The code is based on an existing sample implementation in the Windows Vista version of the Windows SDK. For reference, the existing sample can be found in the Samples\NetDs\NAP subdirectory of a default SDK installation.

The Registry SHA/SHV sample that is described herein builds upon the original SDK sample in the following ways:

- Auto-remediation

- Server-side configuration user interface

- Build and test with run-time security enhancements

Auto-Remediation

As mentioned previously, auto-remediation is an important feature of NAP, wherein unhealthy clients can automatically be brought into compliance by the underlying plug-in implementation without requiring error-prone, end-user intervention.

For example, suppose that the Registry SHA and SHV have been configured to monitor the fictitious registry value EnableSecureMode that is located at HKEY_LOCAL_MACHINE\Software\Contoso. The system administrators want to enforce that only clients that have that value present and set to 1 (enabled) are able to acquire an IP address with DHCP.

What happens in the code when a client that lacks that registry value attempts to obtain an IP address? In order to answer that question, there are a few abstraction layers to be aware of in the sample SHA. The sample SHA implements the INapSystemHealthAgentCallback (see napsystemhealthagent.h in the Windows SDK) via its ShaCallback class (see sha\exe\callback.cpp). Also, to simplify interacting with the registry, and to allow that code to be shared between the SHA and SHV, a helper class that is named CRegistryKeyValue is used (see sdkcommon\src\sdkcommon.cpp).

When the sample SHA's host service starts (see sha\exe\shasvc.cpp), it immediately reads its current registry policy values (using ShaCallback::Init). It then registers for change notifications for each target registry key (by using ShaCallback::ListenRegChange).

Subsequently, when the NAP client queries the registry SHA for a SoH request, the target registry values are serialized into a byte array that can be interpreted by the SHV. On the client, the following call stack shows how this serialization is accomplished:

```
CRegistryKeyValue::Serialize
ShaCallback::Poll
ShaCallback::FillSoHRequest
ShaCallback::GetSoHRequest
```

The SHV uses a similar architecture, wherein the helper CSampleShv class (see shv\sampleshv.cpp) implements the INapSystemHealthValidator interface (from the public header, napsystemhealthvalidator.h). After the SoH request and embedded serialized registry-setting information are received by the SHV that is using CSampleShv::Validate, it deserializes the registry data and compares each value against the expected setting.

However, as a performance enhancement, the bulk of the sample SHV validate implementation is asynchronous. This allows the host NPS to achieve greater throughput across multiple SHV plug-ins. The following call stack shows how this check is accomplished:

```
CRegistryKeyValue::ExtractData (followed by ::MatchedKey)
CSampleShv::CheckRequestSoHHealth
CSampleShv::HandleRequestSoH
CSampleShv::QShvRespondSHVHost
CSampleShv::AsyncThreadHandlerMain
CSampleShv::AsyncThreadHandler
```

In this example, because the client workstation is lacking a required registry value, the preceding call to CheckRequestSoHealth in the SHV results in a status of QUAR_E_NOTPATCHED. The CheckRequestSoHHealth function also serializes the expected values corresponding to the client registry locations that were determined to be noncompliant. This serialized output can be thought of as the remediation instructions for the client.

The resulting status is then returned by HandleRequestSoH (refer again to the preceding call stack), at which point QShvRespondSHVHost calls

::HandleResponseSoH, which in turn calls ::FillResponseSoH to attach the serialized remediation instructions to the SoH response.

Next, the SoH response is returned by NAP to the registry SHA on the client. In this example, the SHA must notify the NAP client that, per instructions that are received from the SHV, remediation actions are now pending. As a result, ProcessSoHResponse calls HandleSoHResponse, which sets a return status of FIXESINPROGRESS.

As an aside, note that an SHA implementation could also determine a noncompliant status in which auto-remediation would not be performed (that is, something requiring direct user intervention to fix). In that case, FIXESNEEDED would be returned instead.

The SHA remediation interface is driven by ::GetFixupInfo, which is the next interface call that is made by the NAP client. Because health-remediation patches are to be applied in this example, GetFixupInfo calls ShaCallback::DoPatch, which will validate the registry information that is returned by the SHV and call CRegistryKeyValue::SetTargetValue to make the mandated correction to the example EnableSecureMode value under HKEY_LOCAL_MACHINE\Software\Contoso. Thus, the client system is patched and may now obtain an IP address.

Finally, it's worth noting that the NAP client interface allows helpful messages to be displayed to the user via a pop-up window in the notification area. As an example, see how the FixupInfo structure (from the public naptypes.h) is populated, following successful remediation in GetFixupInfo.

```
FixupInfo * pStatus
...
pStatus->fixupMsgId = MSG_ID_FIXUP_SUCCESS;
pStatus->percentage = 100;
pStatus->state = fixupStateSuccess;
```

That particular code block informs the NAP client that the client was successfully patched and causes the resource string that corresponds to MSG_ID_FIXUP_SUCCESS to be shown briefly in a notification message, so that the user knows what's going on behind the scenes. Other SHA implementations should take advantage of this mechanism in order to keep the user informed of important state changes (including failure cases, such as an unhealthy client and/or patching fails).

Server-Side Configuration User Interface

The preceding auto-remediation walkthrough section mentions that the CSampleShv class implements the NAP INapSystemHealthValidator interface. Observe in shv\sampleshv.h that the CSampleShv class also implements the INapComponentConfig interface.

The INapComponentConfig interface is an important consideration for SHV implementers, because it exposes a mechanism for the system administrator to configure an SHV by using whatever user interface is appropriate, while still maintaining a common management environment across all SHVs.

The sample Registry SHV includes an implementation of that interface (see shv\sampleshv.cpp!CSampleShv::InvokeUI). To see this interface at work, perform the following steps:

1. Configure a Windows Server 2008 (Beta) machine with the Network Policy and Access Services role.

2. Copy **RegistrySHV.dll** to the System32 directory.

3. Run **regsvr32.exe RegistrySHV.dll**

4. Click **Start**, click **Run**, type **nps.msc**, and then click **OK**.

5. In the console tree (left pane), expand **Network Access Protection**, and then expand **System Health Validators**.

6. In the details pane (right pane), right-click **Sample Registry SHV**, and then click **Properties**.

7. Click **Configure**. You'll see the window shown in Figure 10, which is created by the Registry SHV.

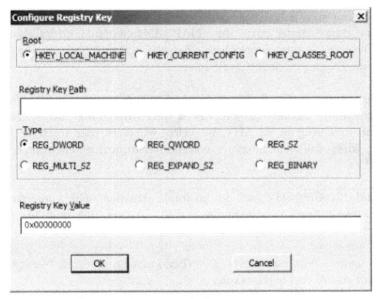

Figure 10 Configure Registry Key window

Implementation Security

Inherent in their architecture and role is the fact that the various components of NAP will be exposed to data from the network. This potentially includes data that is received via an un-encrypted channel over the Internet. This observation is intended simply to reinforce the fact that all code—particularly system-level code, written in Visual C++, exposed to untrusted network data—must be reviewed and made to be as robust as possible.

To this end, the sample Registry SHA and SHV have been configured and tested with the following compile-, link-, and run-time protections in place. More detail about these options is available online and in *Writing Secure Code for Windows Vista* by Howard and LeBlanc.

- Use the strsafe.h routines where appropriate, instead of the potentially riskier CRT alternatives. See Using the Strsafe.h Functions in the MSDN Library (http://tinyurl.com/99bsoy3)

- Enable process termination on heap corruption. See HeapSetInformation Function in the MSDN Library (http://tinyurl.com/94fgng2)

- Compile clean with Warning Level 4 (/W4 /WX)

- Enable Address Space Layout Randomization (linker directive /dynamicbase)

- Enable No-Execute (linker directive /NXCOMPAT. See /NXCOMPAT (Compatible with Data Execution Prevention) in the MSDN Library (http://tinyurl.com/9mmhzvu)

- Enable Safe Structured Exception Handling (linker directive /SAFESEH. See /SAFESEH (Image has Safe Exception Handlers) in the MSDN Library (http://tinyurl.com/9qpc84y)

Operational Security Considerations

When implementing and/or deploying NAP plug-ins, it's important to be aware of two security considerations: remediation and client trust. These should not be construed as design flaws, but instead as limitations of the environment in which NAP must operate.

Remediation

NAP plug-ins that implement auto-remediation should take into account the fact that not all NAP scenarios can guarantee a trusted path between the NAP client and the NPS.

DHCP is an example of a NAP scenario in which remediation data is not protected by a cryptographic integrity check. As a result, it's possible in that scenario that an attacker could modify the SoH response data en route from the SHV, and that the SHA would blindly apply changes that could actually compromise the security of the client.

There are two potential mitigations to this situation. The first is that SHAs should be implemented in such a way that, if they can auto-remediate, they include logic to determine if a requested setting is worse than what's already present. Of course, that's not always possible (the sample Registry SHA is a good example of how hard that logic can be to implement in a general way). Thus, the second potential mitigation is simply not to deploy auto-remediation plug-ins in NAP scenarios that don't guarantee trusted path.

NAP scenarios that do implement a secure channel include IPsec, 801.1x, and VPN.

Client Trust

The second security consideration of the NAP operational environment is that the client is implicitly trusted by NPS. To take an example, suppose that the Registry SHV returns remediation instructions to set the fictitious EnableSecureMode registry value that was described earlier. Suppose further that the client workstation is one on which the end user has local administrator rights. In this example, the end user has installed a custom SHA that looks and acts just like the sample Registry SHA, except that it silently discards remediation changes. As a result, the NAP client reports that patching has occurred, and the client is deemed healthy, even though it's actually not. The NPS has no way to determine otherwise.

The usual security mantra applies here: only give administrator-access to trustworthy users, and only to the machines where the users truly need it. However, some NAP scenarios, such as VPN, are inherently mobile-user-oriented, in which case the client is likely a laptop. Historically, laptop users have required administrator access; otherwise they risk not being able to make certain unforeseen configuration changes while they travel. Thus, those users have the level of access that is required to make the kinds of changes that could compromise the NAP client.

18 SECURING YOUR PASSWORDS

You may be surprised to hear the following security recommendation: write all of your passwords down on a sheet of paper and put them in your purse or wallet. But this is one of the best security practices around. Why? Because here's what you don't want to do:

- Use the same or similar passwords on multiple sites

- Use easy-to-remember passwords

- Keep the same password for more than a few months

Given the number of different online accounts that the average user maintains these days (Facebook, bank, email, etc.), it's almost impossible to meet those guidelines without writing the passwords down. But the worst place to write them down is in a file stored on your computer hard disk, where it can be found by a hacker or by malware, regardless of how well you think it's hidden. The one place malware can't reach? A sheet of paper. And the best place to put that sheet of paper so you don't lose it is in your wallet.

Passwords can be a big security and manageability headache for enterprise IT administrators. Users often create simple passwords to make sure that they'll remember them. In addition, there are few secure and efficient procedures for resetting passwords.

Even with these limitations, you can mitigate these types of security problems when remote users access your network. First, you could use certificate authorities to issue certificates to your users, but this requires a public key infrastructure (PKI) and is expensive to set up and maintain. It can also be difficult to manage certificates for remote users, especially if you are using a hardware-based token, such as a smartcard. This kind of trade-off of high cost for high security is a common theme. Alternatively, you could use SecureID, which is the OTP solution from RSA. However, you should note that SecureID is not based on a standard, which can cause incompatibilities and licensing overhead.

A third option is to use a standards-based OTP solution. The following chapter covers how to use standards-based technologies with C# and C to develop a one-time password (OTP) proof of concept, and explains why an OTP is better than traditional passwords.

19 ONE-TIME PASSWORDS

A traditional, static password is usually only changed when necessary: either when it has expired or when the user has forgotten it and needs to reset it. Because passwords are cached on computer hard drives and stored on servers, they are susceptible to cracking. This is especially a concern for laptops since they can be easily stolen.

Many businesses give employees laptops and open their networks to remote access. They also hire temporary employees and vendors. In this environment, a simple static password solution can become a liability.

Unlike a static password, a one-time password (OTP) changes each time the user logs in. The passwords themselves are generated in one of two ways: either as time-synchronized or counter-synchronized. Both approaches typically require the user to carry a small hardware device (often on a key chain) that is synchronized with a server, and both typically use some algorithm to generate the password.

Time-synchronized OTPs are widely deployed but are subject to problems caused by clock skew. That is, if the authentication server and the user token don't keep the same time, then the expected OTP value won't be produced and the user authentication will fail. With time-synchronized OTPs, the user typically must enter the password within a certain period of time before it's considered expired and another one must be generated.

A counter-synchronized OTP solution synchronizes a counter between the client device and the server. The counter is advanced each time an OTP value is requested of the device. Just like with time-synchronized OTPs, when the user wants to log on, he or she enters the OTP that is currently displayed on the device.

Challenge-based OTPs are a special case and also often use a hardware device. However, the user must provide a known value, such as a personal identification number (PIN), to cause the OTP to be generated. This type of OTP is currently being rolled out in Europe to add authentication to credit and debit cards. The OTP solutions in use today are all built on some sort of cryptographic processing to generate the current password from a synchronization parameter (that is, the time or counter value), a secret key, and possibly a PIN.

ONE-TIME PASSWORDS

For example, hash-based OTPs use cryptographic hashing algorithms to compute the password, a one-way function that maps an arbitrary length message to a fixed-length digest. Thus, a hash-based OTP starts with the inputs (synchronization parameter, secret key, and PIN), runs them through the one-way function, and produces the fixed-length password.

So which method should you choose? The following sample solution details how to create counter-synchronized OTPs using IIS 7.0 and keyed-hash message authentication, as described in the RFC 2104 (http://tinyurl.com/6ktdm9) and RFC 4426 (http://tinyurl.com/9ngkxf2) standards.

OTP Sample Solution

Because this is a sample solution, you'll use a simple client application to create the OTPs. In the real world, you would want to integrate this with a tamper-resistant hardware device.

In order to build this OTP solution, you need to create a standards-based OTP authentication web service that is backed by SQL Server and integrated into ASP.NET. You'll create an OTP generator that is installed on each client computer, which users will run to generate a new OTP.

The user types the OTP value when prompted by the web browser, and then clicks Submit to authenticate. The OTP plug-in module is notified by IIS and subsequently calls the web service to verify authentication attempts. The web service looks up the user's key and counter value in the SQL Server table, verifies the OTP computation, and responds with authentication success or failure.

Figure 11 shows the architecture of the sample solution. Keep in mind that in a production environment, this architecture should be further hardened against denial of service (DoS) attacks by actions such as configuring a trust relationship between the client and server, and throttling invalid logon attempts.

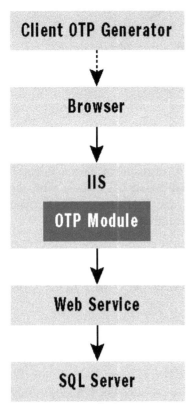

Figure 11 OTP solution components

The sample code provided by MSDN Magazine (http://tinyurl.com/c3oedvu) consists of a Visual Studio 2005 solution that includes a C++ DLL to generate the OTP (HmacOtpDll). Because this DLL is used by the OtpClient and the web service, you can put it into the system32 folder. (You can use a post-build event to automatically copy it there.) The sample also includes a console application called OtpClient that generates the OTP value. OtpClient uses an XML file to store the secret code and counter. Every time the application is rebuilt, it copies the XML from the project root to the target directory, causing the counter to reset to 0.

An IIS module (called IIS7Module) provides OTP authentication services, and a web service (called WebService) is used by the module to verify the OTP value. The web service contains a SQL Server Express database, which is located in App_Data. Finally, web pages are included in the TestWebsite project, which is used for testing the solution.

Test OTP Generator Client

The test OTP generator client application is a self-contained tool that allows users to obtain OTP authentication values. It takes the place of a hardware device plus the challenge (such as a PIN request) that would typically be required in a real deployment. To compute OTPs, this client component uses a DLL that is shared with the authentication web service. For the purpose of this sample application, the user runs the tool to create the next OTP and then manually types that value into a form in a web browser. All of this is done using C# and some C. (C is chosen for the low-level implementation of the OTP cryptography.)

You've seen how OTPs work at a user level, but how does this solution work at a functional level? This hash-based OTP solution takes two values as input: a key and a count. However, an OTP solution also has metadata relevant to the implementer, including the length of the key and the length of the expected OTP value that the user has to type when authenticating.

This sample produces OTPs that are six characters in length, and can support up to eight characters. For the sake of simplicity, this implementation uses some fixed-length buffers that limit the key length to 64 bytes. However, assuming that the key is a high-quality, cryptographically random number, that's a huge key space. Such a key would not be the weak link in a production deployment. (A typical size for a random key today is 256 bits, or 32 bytes.)

The count value increments each time an authentication attempt is made by a given user (or technically, with a given key). The security of the OTP solution depends upon the count value never being reused; this is enforced by the OTP server. In this implementation, the count is a 64-bit unsigned integer. As discussed earlier, another way to deploy this would be to use time synchronization with a server.

A keyed hash message authentication code (HMAC) is a key-based cryptographic hash. Or to put it another way, an HMAC takes an arbitrary message and a key and maps the message to a fixed-size digest value (e.g. 20 bytes), ensuring that only someone with the same key can produce the same digest value from the same message.

The first computational step for HMAC-OTP is to take the count value and encode it as the input message for an HMAC computation. In this implementation, the message is an 8-byte buffer set to the counter value. Figure 12 depicts this and the following two steps. The next computational step is to compute the HMAC of the above message with the user's key. Note that this solution addresses byte ordering in order ensure that it is compliant with the RFCs.

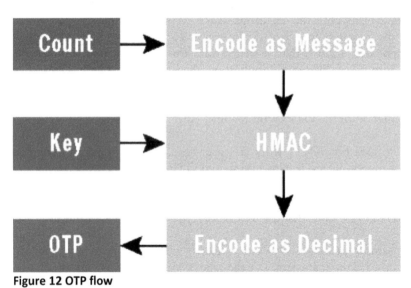

Figure 12 OTP flow

The 20-byte HMAC result is then turned into the OTP value, which is accomplished by making a decimal encoding of the HMAC result. There are two practical requirements here: first, you need to preserve as many bits of the HMAC computation as possible, up to the length of the OTP result (six numbers in this case), since losing bits exposes the computation to

THE FOUR PILLARS OF ENDPOINT SECURITY

cryptographic attack. Second, you need to create an OTP that is compatible with as many varieties of input devices as possible. This compatibility requirement is why this solution implements decimal encoding. (This strong-authentication implementation is even compatible with a rotary phone!)

The Sample Website

The goal is to ensure that the site is designed to show whether users have successfully or unsuccessfully logged in using OTPs. In order to facilitate testing, the OTP solution includes a sample website. The first page in the site is Default.htm, a landing page for authenticated users that demonstrates how even non-ASP.NET pages are protected by the OTP module. Included is Test.aspx, a file that shows the currently authenticated user name, as well as Test.aspx.cs, a file that shows how the Test.aspx page retrieves the authenticated username from the System.Web.UI.Page.User property. Also included in the solution are a web.config file that includes a reference to OtpModule, and a Visual Studio project solution with a reference to the IISModule.dll file.

The IIS HTTP OTP plug-in module is a component of the website. The module interfaces with IIS and redirects users to a web form where they can enter their usernames and OTPs. When a user submits a username and OTP, the module validates the input and redirects the user to the appropriate success or failure page. The module also pairs the authentication status of the user with the user's session.

For maintainability and supportability, this module is managed, so it's written in C#. The plug-in module is a client of the authentication web service, which is discussed next.

The OTP module implements the IHttpModule interface. In fact, the module is remarkably simple and consists of only three public methods. The first is Init, as shown here:

```
public void Init(HttpApplication application)

{

    application.BeginRequest                +=              new
EventHandler(application_BeginRequest);

}
```

As you can see, the module uses this method to register its BeginRequest handler, application_BeginRequest. The purpose of the OTP BeginRequest handler is to ensure that all HTTP requests are made by an authenticated user. This is accomplished by using a few helper functions: one to determine whether the caller is authenticated and a few others to perform the authentication if the caller is not already authenticated. It is also worth mentioning here that intercepting the request during the BeginRequest event does not follow the standard authentication pattern used by ASP.NET applications. This approach is recommended, however, if you don't want other modules to see the request, even those that, by design, want to intercept requests prior to authentication.

The IsAuthenticated helper function determines if the request indicates an authenticated user. This is done by checking the application context for a properly encrypted authentication cookie using the classes HttpContext, HttpCookie, and Security.FormsAuthenticationTicket within the System.Web namespace. If the cookie is present and decrypts without error, the caller is deemed to be authenticated. Otherwise, there are two possible states: either this is an OTP authentication request that should be processed, or the web client request is invalid (unauthenticated) and a login form is displayed.

The OTP module includes a built-in login form known as LoginPage.htm. It consists of five HTML elements: an initially empty error message field, a username field, a password field, a Submit button, and a hidden input field named hdLoginForm.

If the caller is already authenticated, the module takes no further action. Accordingly, the request continues to process. In this solution, the Default.htm page is loaded.

If the caller isn't authenticated, the IsAuthenticationPost helper function is called. It checks whether the request type is POST and if the request form has the hdLoginForm input field. The method returns true if both conditions are confirmed.

If the request is an authentication request, the TryAuthenticate helper function is called. The username and OTP values are retrieved from the request context and passed to the authentication web service's VerifyOtpCode method. If the verification is successful, a new encrypted authentication cookie is attached to the response. The response is then redirected to the default page (Default.htm). One way to extend this solution is to save the original page requested by the user and redirect the user to that page following a successful authentication.

If the VerifyOtpCode web service call fails, the request is redirected back to the login form, which now displays an error message, and the helper function ShowLoginForm is called. The helper function loads the login page from the resource section of the module, sets the error message string in the page (if appropriate), and sets the login page as the response to the current request. It then signals the request as complete (this happens regardless of the nature of the request).

The Authentication Web Service

The authentication web service is responsible for performing the actual OTP authentication by determining whether the provided OTP value demonstrates that the named user has knowledge of the secret key.

The implementation of the OTP authentication web service is quite simple since it reuses the low-level cryptographic library, which implements the OTP computation discussed in the earlier section on the test OTP generator client. This reuse comes in the form of a P/Invoke call to the GenerateOTP export of the native HmacOtpDll.dll.

The web service exposes a single web method, VerifyOtpCode, which returns true for a successful authentication. The first step in that method is to load the SQL Server row corresponding to the username indicated in the authentication request. If SQL Server cannot find a matching row, the method returns false.

If the username is found in the SQL Server database, the following data items are passed to the native GenerateOTP: the OTP value that is specified in the request, the secret key for the user (retrieved from SQL Server), and a counter value (also retrieved from SQL Server).

GenerateOTP is retried with sequential counter values until either it returns a matching OTP value or until, at most, 1,000 sequential counter values have been checked. That allows for the user to have accidentally advanced the client counter offline, although that's admittedly unlikely to have happened 1,000 times since the last successful authentication!

Reducing this range would also reduce the already unlikely chance that an attacker might actually guess an OTP value that happens to be in the sequence, but it increases the possibility that the user may accidentally advance the client counter beyond the range attempted by the server. In the latter case, administrator intervention is required in order for the user to authenticate again.

If a matching OTP value is found within the counter range, the new counter value is written back to the database. While that unfortunately requires the authentication web service to have write-access to the database, it's also critical to the security of the OTP since, as described previously, a counter value must never be reused. (For the OTP to be unique, it really must only be used one time.)

A SQL Server database with a simple schema is used to store usernames and their corresponding OTP secret key or seed value. You can also extend the schema to include logging information, such as the number and times of successful and unsuccessful log-on attempts using the OTP. The database consists of the Username, SecretCode, and Counter columns. The copy of the database that accompanies the sample code has only one row for the username, testuser.

The Complete Architecture

Figure 13 shows what the solution looks like when it's complete. As you can see, the user launches the client application, generates an OTP, then navigates to the authentication web application, and pastes the OTP into the web browser form. The form is generated by the OTP module when it detects that the request isn't authenticated. When the user clicks Submit, the web browser form sends the request to the server where it's again intercepted by the OTP module. Next, the OTP module calls the OTP web service to verify the user authentication data. Finally, if successful, the web server calls the handler for the requested page, which could be of any type (HTML, ASP.NET, PHP, and so on).

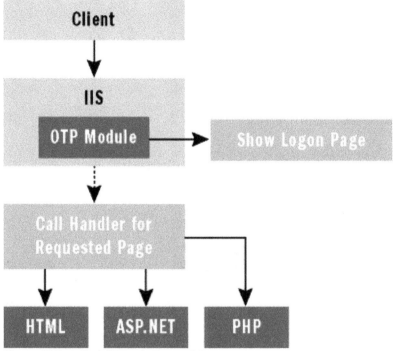

Figure 13 Detailed OTP solution architecture

Running the Code Sample

To run the code sample, you'll need Windows Vista or Windows Server 2008 with IIS 7.0 (with the Application Server role enabled for Windows Server 2008), Visual Studio 2005, SQL Server 2005 or SQL Server Express, and the OTP sample code. For experimenting with the sample solution, it's recommended that you use Windows Server 2008 and SQL Server Express, since that's what is used here. In the following description, assume that the OTP sample code solution file is located at C:\Test\OTP\Otp.sln.

To prepare your environment, install the IIS module using either the IIS Manager or by editing the web.config file. Enable read and write access to C:\Test\OTP\webservice\app_data for either the IIS_IUSRS account or the account configured as the identity for a custom application pool. Then add a website for OtpTest and OtpService.

Registering the IIS module using the web.config file (this step has already been completed in the sample—see TestWebsite\Web.Config) requires the following configuration markup:

```
<system.webServer>

  modules>

    <add name="OtpModule" type="OtpModule" />

  </modules>

</system.webServer>
```

You should also add the module DLL to the bin folder or the global assembly cache (GAC). To register the OTP module DLL with the GAC, use a command such as the following:

```
gacutil.exe /i iis7module.dll
```

To use IIS Manager, open it and click on the name of your computer in the console tree. In the middle pane, double-click the **Modules** icon, and then click **Add Managed Module** in the actions pane. Next, select **OtpModule** from the dropdown list. If you put the DLL into the GAC and you're using IIS Manager to add the module, then you might need to restart IIS in order to refresh the modules list.

In order to properly increment the number-of-attempts value in SQL Server Express, the NETWORK SERVICE account requires read and write access to the C:\Test\Otp\WebService\App_Data directory. The required permissions for this object are read and execute, list folder contents, read, and write, as shown in Figure 14.

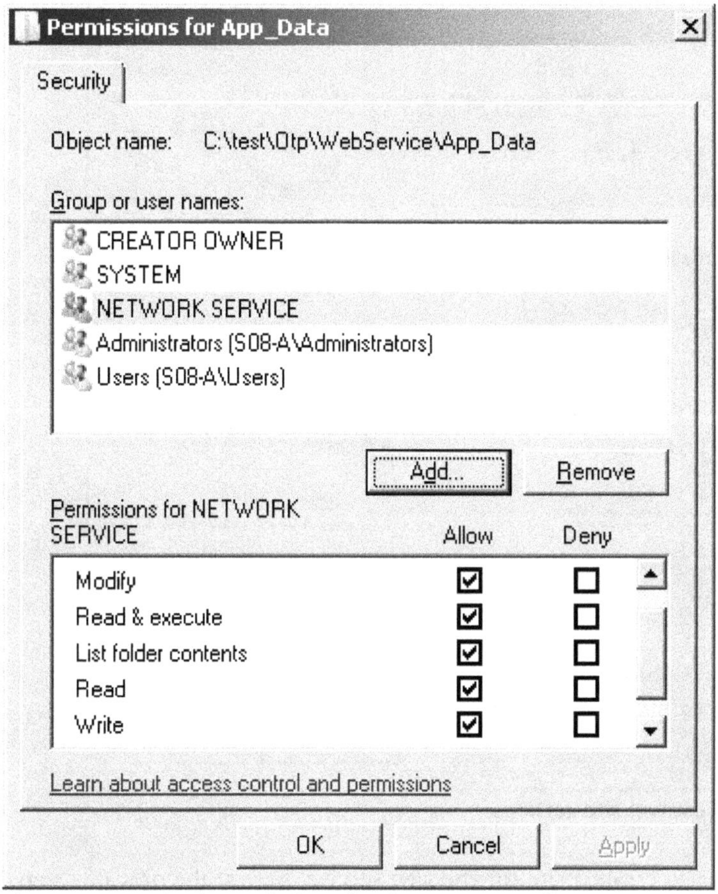

Figure 14 Required permissions for the App_Data directory

You must also set up a site in IIS for the test website. To do this, open the IIS Manager console, and in the ISS Manager console tree, expand the node with your computer's name, right-click **Sites**, and then click **Add Web Site**. Use the following settings for your new site, and then click **OK**.

- Site name: OtpTest

- Physical path: C:\test\Otp\TestWebsite

- Port: 8000

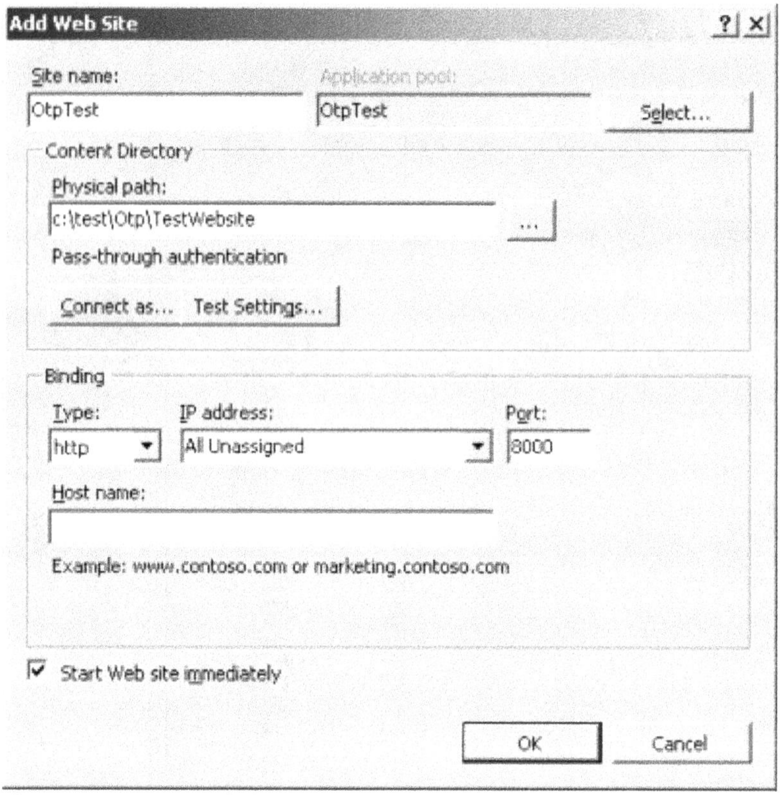

Figure 15 OtpTest website settings

You must also create a site for the web service. Repeat the previous steps, using the following settings:

- Site name: OtpService

- Physical path: C:\Test\Otp\WebService

- Port: 8080

Next, open the Otp.sln solution in Visual Studio, expand **IIS7Module** in the solution explorer, expand **Web References**, right-click **OtpService**, click **Properties**, and then confirm that the Web Reference URL is set to http://localhost:8080/service.asmx. In the Build menu, click **Build Solution** and confirm that no build errors have occurred.

Now you should test to ensure that the OTP module has been properly registered and loads correctly. To do so, navigate to **http://localhost:8000**

and verify that you see a page that looks like the logon page shown in Figure 16. To test the implementation, type **testuser** in the Username field.

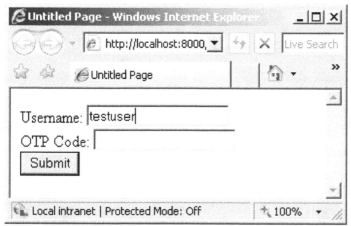

Figure 16 Logon page of test website

To get the value for the OTP Code textbox, open a Command Prompt Window as an administrator and navigate to the build directory of the OTP client program (C:\Test\Otp\otpclient\bin\debug). Run OtpClient.exe to get the next OTP value. You should see something like that shown in Figure 17.

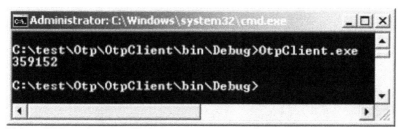

Figure 17 Running OtpClient.exe to get OTP value

Type the OTP value into the OTP Code textbox, and then click **Submit**. Figure 18 shows the sample OTP code in the page. If the authentication is successful, you are directed to the Default.htm page.

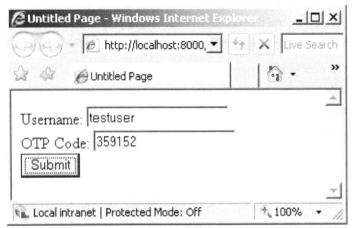

Figure 18 Test page with sample OTP value

Click the **Text.aspx link** on the default page to go to a demo page, which displays the name of the currently authenticated user (if any). If the authentication credentials were incorrect, you should see the error message shown in Figure 19.

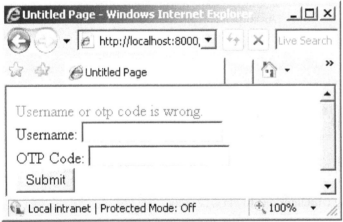

Figure 19 Error message shown when authentication is unsuccessful

Deployment Considerations

If you were to deploy this sample solution in a real-world environment, there are a number of items that you would want to consider. Real deployments store the user key/seed in a tamper-resistant device, such as hardware tokens. It is recommended that you modify the solution to lock the account in response to too many consecutive failed authentication attempts.

You can do this by adding SQL Server columns and a feature to the web service.

If interoperability is a concern, it is recommended that you perform interoperability testing on the low-level HMAC code. Also realize that the MD5 hash algorithm is no longer considered secure. It's used in this sample solution in order to run some basic Known-Vector Tests with what's available in the RFC documents. But a deployable solution should use one of the SHA-2 algorithms to create the hashes.

When developing more user-friendly authentication pages, be sure not to distinguish between bad username and bad password. Otherwise, you're letting attackers learn valid usernames. You'll also need some sort of provisioning solution for adding and removing users or perhaps synchronizing the authentication database with another repository, such as Active Directory.

If you are just targeting ASP.NET, the module could have been implemented as a standard ASP.NET HTTP module. However, such a solution would only secure .aspx files. Note that the IHttpModule interface is the same whether you are configuring it with the ASP.NET runtime or IIS 7.0, so if an original solution was an ASP.NET-specific module, then enabling it to support all file types is a simple change in configuration.

You can use Visual Studio for editing the database. To edit the database, go to the Solution Explorer tree view, expand **WebService**, expand **App_Data**, and select **Open** from the context menu. In the Server Explorer panel that appears, expand **Data Connections**, expand **otp.mdf**, expand **Tables**, right-click **Users**, and then click **Show Table Data**.

Figure 20 shows the table data in the Visual Studio IDE. Just be sure not to leave the database open in the IDE when testing; the web service won't be able to open it and the authentication will fail.

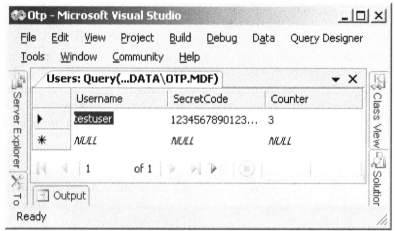

Figure 20 OTP solution components

CONCLUSION

20 ECONOMICS AND RISK

"Security adds hassle and blocks progress..."

"Tight security usually leads first to paralysis and then to weak security, which no one complains about until there is a crisis."

- Butler W. Lampson

It has become something of a cliché in the IT world to say that there is a trade-off between security and usability on the Internet. Every site seems to have its own password and username restrictions, usually in an attempt to make the user's experience more secure. Psychological studies have shown that most people can easily remember one to two username and password combinations. However, three or more combinations make it exceedingly more difficult for people to remember and manage the credentials.

There is almost no chance that users can keep all of their identity needs straight, let alone stick to stringent security policies while still completing the task that sent them to the Internet in the first place. Many solutions have been proposed: smartcards, biometrics, and single sign-on programs. However, none of these options have provided more than isolated improvements.

USABILITY VS. SECURITY

USABLE   LESS USABLE   BALANCED   LESS SECURE   SECURE

Security is About Economics

Security is a balance between the expected benefit of loss prevention versus its real cost. This includes deploying and maintaining hardware and software that blocks attacks that seek to create those losses, and also the time spent by users remembering or recovering passwords, or finding a workaround that allows them to do their jobs. Most security is too difficult for users who have little incentive to cooperate with a hassle that blocks their ability to get their work done. This is completely rational behavior by users who perceive the cost of security to be too high given the time that it takes away from productive work. By the same token, trying to educate users on good security practices in the face of the clear and present cost to them of complying with security directives is not time well spent.

The best security solutions are those in which the question, "Is this Usable Security?" can be answered, "Yes, really!" That answer needs to be supported by metrics generated both during normal operations and by user feedback, and the solution needs to support producing those metrics that not only prove the efficacy of deployed product, but also help continuous improvement.

Best Practice—Gathering and Analyzing Usability Metrics

The following notes apply to metrics that can be generated by user input, either during the operation of the task, or later using feedback from a variety of channels.

- The best feedback comes from the user at the time that they are frustrated.

- Always allow the user to send feedback on a task as it completes.

- Radio-button feedback takes the least user effort and therefore has the best volume.

- Text boxes in which users can explain the problem are the most helpful.

- The most expensive feedback is from focus groups or user interviews.

Metrics that can be generated automatically for comparison between new and experienced users to determine how clear each task and decision point is, include:

- Time to complete specific tasks.

- Time at each decision page.

- Fall-off at each decision page and for the entire task.

- Whether the user needs to stop a task and return later, for longer term operations.

These data should be a part of the normal data collection along with server statistics.

The goal is to marry the determination of whether the security is usable with "design for test" principles. That way, the design of the schema, data collection, and even the application itself will include the information needed to get real usability metrics from the operation of the delivered solution. This should happen both during beta testing and in the field. The results drive improvements to subsequent versions of the product.

Below are some interesting reports on usable security:

- "Usable Security: How to Get It" by Butler Lampson (http://tinyurl.com/8qm64g3)

- "An Economic View of Usable Security" (a video on 10 years of research at UCL) (http://tinyurl.com/9quf86n)

Managing Risk

Protecting information assets is best done in a way that balances usability, technology cost, and the value of the asset. This balance reflects *calculated* risk, where threat modeling and analysis are critical steps in achieving an appropriate balance of risk, and the balance changes over time.

INSIDER THREATS

It's important to remember that all assets face some risk, even from trusted insiders. Two high-profile news stories serve as a reminder of the tough challenges faced by IT managers when mitigating insider threats: WikiLeaks and StuxNet. Both of these stories highlight the potential damage that can be caused, intentionally or unintentionally, by people with privileged access to data and systems.

WikiLeaks

The WikiLeaks case demonstrates how easily an insider can take sensitive information and publish it to a public forum with the intent to discredit or shame an agency or employer. But more generally, the threat is of any sort of unauthorized disclosure (e.g. classified data, software source code, or a customer list), and it's important to note that it can happen maliciously or accidentally.

Mitigating unauthorized disclosure risk can be a major effort involving the time-consuming and frequently ambiguous process of:

- Locating and classifying data.

- Determining who has access to that data, who should have access, how, and when.

- Instituting the necessary access controls for enforcement.

- Auditing access and archiving logs.

Even so, discretionary access controls don't protect the organization against rogue insiders who are authorized to access certain information but not to disclose it externally. Some additional protection is afforded by commercial Data Loss Prevention (DLP) technologies, but it is infeasible to guard against every possible way that sensitive data can be disclosed (http://tinyurl.com/ygkyjld). The importance of the human element, including instituting periodic vetting of personnel in a manner commensurate with the risk, cannot be overlooked. You also must not underestimate the importance of being prepared in advance to respond to a disclosure incident when one occurs. Having a mitigation and communication plan in place for such an incident can be crucial for reducing hits to your organization's reputation.

StuxNet

StuxNet (http://tinyurl.com/2vol5nk) makes an interesting contrast to the WikiLeaks story for two reasons. First, it reinforces the point that the insider can be innocent, albeit careless. While it's unclear to what extent user carelessness played a role in the propagation of StuxNet, the takeaway is clear: a trusted user can, for example, introduce an infected USB key into the vulnerable internal LAN. User education is crucial.

StuxNet also reminds us of the importance of two parallel efforts that, only when applied together, can help ensure a higher level of organizational security.

1. **IT organization**—Configuring the environment and software in a secure manner.

2. **Software developers and vendors**—Keeping the Security Development Lifecycle (SDL) practices in mind when developing applications.

When working on a secure IT infrastructure, the main objective of most enterprises is to maintain seamless business continuity. However, the evolution of the line-of-business needs of a typical organization has resulted in an enterprise network perimeter that is completely permeable. This is due to the proliferation of web applications, remote productivity solutions, and a geographically distributed workforce using bring-your-own-device (BYOD) hardware. Network perimeter permeability allows enterprise networks and their assets to be under constant attack from intruders. In response, IT administrators must continuously test and deploy the latest patches and updated security configuration at the network, server, and application layers. Due to the patch/reboot cycle, plus the ability of attackers to constantly hammer end-user devices, servers, and applications, there's frequently downtime in enterprise environments.

Best Practice—Breaking the Vicious Cycle of Downtime

- Run servers with the minimum required feature set, omitting unnecessary roles and add-ons.

- Pre-test patches to determine which ones are critical, which ones require reboots, and which ones have an alternative workaround.

- Conduct regular penetration testing at the personnel, facility, network, and application layers. Even using a simple checklist for this is better than nothing; the most sophisticated organizations will complement internal expertise with the latest external tools and training.

- Create and maintain a threat model for each service, and use it to prioritize your efforts.

While enterprises often place a lot of emphasis on uptime statistics, network bandwidth is an enterprise-shared resource that is frequently overlooked. A distributed denial of service (DDoS) is one type of attack that can cause bandwidth starvation. However, there are many other conditions that can also cause excessive network load. For example, peer-to-peer file sharing, heavy use of streaming video, and peak heavy usage of an internal or external server (e.g. the retail industry's Black Friday) can all make the network run sluggish both to internal users and external customers.

Many enterprises are becoming dependent on using streaming video for core business operations. For example, geographically distributed companies use it for interoffice communications, brand management companies use it for media campaigns, and the military uses it for command and control.

As businesses have become more dependent on these assorted technologies, the following conditions have resulted in a precarious situation:

- A DDoS type of attack is fairly easy to launch

- The quality and reliability of streaming video is highly dependent on bandwidth availability

- Networks are already heavily loaded, even in optimal cases

IT managers must be prepared to handle the risks associated with these technologies. They need to change their long-term thinking and planning about resource usage, protecting devices on the network, and protecting that critical network bandwidth.

21 FROM FOUR TENETS TO FOUR PILLARS

Given the complexity of modern business communications, it's easy to lose sight of the basics. Having invested the time and energy to understand the risks facing your business, you may find it hard to shift gears and start to look at these risks as opportunities. Remember that your competitors are facing those same challenges, and the solutions that you develop and deploy to mitigate those risks become strategic assets.

IT security is a great example of how risks can be turned into assets that enable greater business velocity and new opportunities. And, as complex as BYOD and cloud computing are, the basic four tenets of IT security still apply:

- Identity

- Authentication

- Access control

- Authorization

Apply those tenets as you make investments across each of the Four Pillars of Endpoint Security:

- Endpoint hardening

- Endpoint reliability

- Network prioritization

- Network reliability

And don't forget the correlation between IT investment, business agility, happy employees, and satisfied customers.

ABOUT THE AUTHOR

Dan Griffin is the founder of JW Secure, a Seattle-based company specializing in custom security software development. Dan is the author of *Cloud Security and Control* and *The Four Pillars of Endpoint Security*, is a frequent conference speaker, and is a Microsoft Enterprise Security MVP.

Dan holds a Master's degree in Computer Science from the University of Washington and a Bachelor's degree in Computer Science from Indiana University.

www.ingramcontent.com/pod-product-compliance
Lightning Source LLC
Chambersburg PA
CBHW071222050326
40689CB00011B/2415